To Felicity and Claire Linnemann.

ALTHORP

THE STORY OF AN ENGLISH HOUSE

Charles Spencer

Charles Spencer.

7th August, 2000.

VIKING

VIKING

Published by the Penguin Group
Penguin Books Ltd, 27 Wrights Lane, London w8 5tz, England
Penguin Putnam Inc., 375 Hudson Street, New York, New York 10014, USA
Penguin Books Australia Ltd, Ringwood, Victoria, Australia
Penguin Books Canada Ltd, 10 Alcorn Avenue, Toronto, Ontario, Canada m4v 3b2
Penguin Books (NZ) Ltd, Private Bag 102902, NSMC, Auckland, New Zealand
Penguin Books Ltd, Registered Offices: Harmondsworth, Middlesex, England

First published 1998
1 3 5 7 9 10 8 6 4 2

Set in 12 on 15pt Monotype Baskerville
Designed in QuarkXpress on an Apple Macintosh
Printed in Great Britain by Butler & Tanner Ltd, Frome and London

A CIP catalogue record for this book is available from the British Library

isbn 0–670–88322–0

The publishers would like to thank the following for providing photographs
and for permission to reproduce copyright material. While every effort
has been made to trace and acknowledge copyright holders, we would like
to apologise for any errors or omissions.

All photographs copyright © Althorp, except for photographs on:
p. 61 © British Architectural Library, RIBA, London; p. 108 from the
Northampton Independent, 1913; p. 154 © Dave Chancellor/Alpha, London;
p. 158 © David Jones/PA News; p. 165 © Jon O'Brien, 1998;
p. 166 © David Jones/PA News; p. 167 © Jon O'Brien, 1998.

For Grandfather, without whom
Althorp would no longer belong to my family,
and, indeed, may not have survived at all.

OWNERS OF ALTHORP

[1500s to 1783]

John Spencer of Hodnell, Co. Warwick,
m. Warsted

John Spencer, feofee of Wormleighton, 1469; lessee of Althorp, 1486

Sir John Spencer, bought Althorp 1508, d. 1522
m. Isabell Graunt

Sir William Spencer, d. 1532
m. Susan Knightley

Sir John Spencer, d. 1586
m. Katherine Kitson

Sir John Spencer, d. 1599
m. 1566, Mary Catlyn

Sir Robert Spencer, created Baron Spencer of Wormleighton, 1603. 1570–1627
m. 1587, Margaret Willoughby, d. 1597

William, 2nd Baron Spencer, KB, 1591–1636
m. 1614, Lady Penelope Wriothesley, 1598–1667

Henry, 3rd Baron Spencer, created Earl of Sunderland, 1643. 1620–1643
m. 1639, Lady Dorothy Sidney, 1617–1684

Robert, 2nd Earl of Sunderland, KG, 1641–1702
m. 1665, Lady Anne Digby, 1646–1715

Charles, 3rd Earl of Sunderland, KG, 1675–1722
m. (1) 1695, Lady Arabella Cavendish, 1673–1698
m. (2) 1699, Lady Anne Churchill, d. 1716
m. (3) 1717, Judith Tichborne, d. 1749

Robert, 4th Earl of Sunderland, 1701–1729*

Charles, 5th Earl of Sunderland, 3rd Duke of Marlborough, KG, 1706–1758. Quitted Althorp 1734*

Hon. John Spencer, 1708–1746*
m. 1734, Lady Georgina Carteret, 1716–1780

John Spencer, created Earl Spencer 1765. 1734–1783
m. 1755, Georgiana Poyntz, 1737–1814

* son of Charles, 3rd Earl of Sunderland and Lady Anne Churchill

OWNERS OF ALTHORP AND THEIR FAMILIES

[1765 to date]

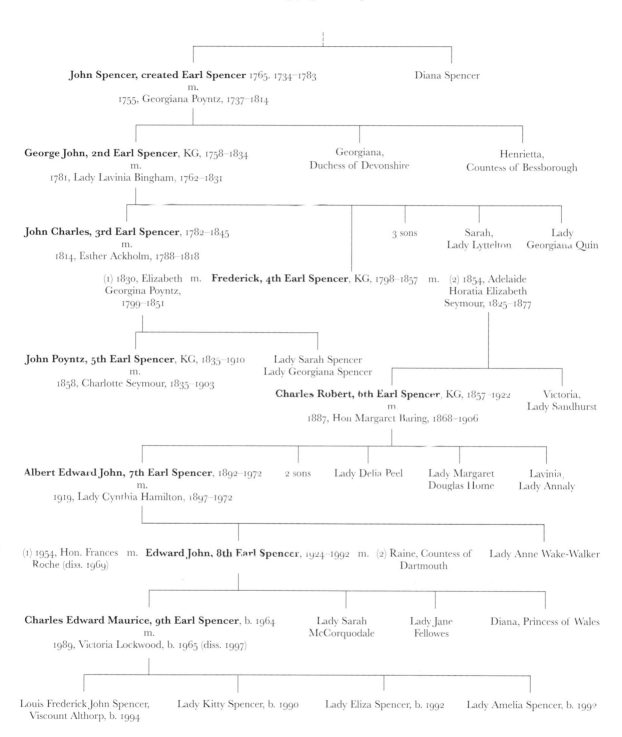

John Spencer, created Earl Spencer 1765. 1734–1783
m.
1755, Georgiana Poyntz, 1737–1814

Diana Spencer

George John, 2nd Earl Spencer, KG, 1758–1834
m.
1781, Lady Lavinia Bingham, 1762–1831

Georgiana,
Duchess of Devonshire

Henrietta,
Countess of Bessborough

John Charles, 3rd Earl Spencer, 1782–1845
m.
1814, Esther Acklom, 1788–1818

3 sons

Sarah,
Lady Lyttelton

Lady
Georgiana Quin

(1) 1830, Elizabeth   m.   **Frederick, 4th Earl Spencer**, KG, 1798–1857   m.   (2) 1854, Adelaide
Georgina Poyntz,   Horatia Elizabeth
1799–1851   Seymour, 1825–1877

John Poyntz, 5th Earl Spencer, KG, 1835–1910
m.
1858, Charlotte Seymour, 1835–1903

Lady Sarah Spencer
Lady Georgiana Spencer

Charles Robert, 6th Earl Spencer, KG, 1857–1922
m.
1887, Hon Margaret Baring, 1868–1906

Victoria,
Lady Sandhurst

Albert Edward John, 7th Earl Spencer, 1892–1972
m.
1919, Lady Cynthia Hamilton, 1897–1972

2 sons

Lady Delia Peel

Lady Margaret
Douglas Home

Lavinia,
Lady Annaly

(1) 1954, Hon. Frances   m.   **Edward John, 8th Earl Spencer**, 1924–1992   m.   (2) Raine, Countess of
Roche (diss. 1969)   Dartmouth

Lady Anne Wake-Walker

Charles Edward Maurice, 9th Earl Spencer, b. 1964
m.
1989, Victoria Lockwood, b. 1965 (diss. 1997)

Lady Sarah
McCorquodale

Lady Jane
Fellowes

Diana, Princess of Wales

Louis Frederick John Spencer,
Viscount Althorp, b. 1994

Lady Kitty Spencer, b. 1990

Lady Eliza Spencer, b. 1992

Lady Amelia Spencer, b. 1992

GROUND- AND FIRST-FLOOR PLANS OF ALTHORP

[not to scale]

GROUND FLOOR

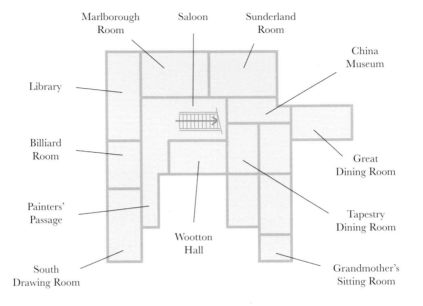

Marlborough Room

Saloon

Sunderland Room

China Museum

Library

Billiard Room

Great Dining Room

Painters' Passage

Tapestry Dining Room

Wootton Hall

South Drawing Room

Grandmother's Sitting Room

FIRST FLOOR

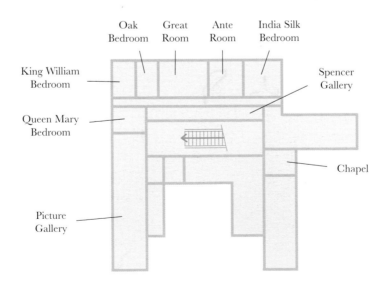

Oak Bedroom

Great Room

Ante Room

India Silk Bedroom

King William Bedroom

Spencer Gallery

Queen Mary Bedroom

Chapel

Picture Gallery

I can't remember exactly when I realized that Althorp would come my way. Certainly I was conscious of the fact by the time of my grandfather's eightieth birthday in 1972, when the local paper in Northamptonshire took a photograph of him, me and my father, and referred to the 'three generations' in rather dynastic terms.

It was an unsettling thought for an introspective and shy little boy: this leviathan of an edifice being my responsibility, my home. I remember a cousin, who had traditionally made no secret of his wish

The three generations, grandfather, father and son.

to lord it at Althorp, looking momentarily optimistic when, aged seven or eight, I declared to him that I would never live there.

My reservations stemmed from two facts: I had not lived there in my early childhood, and could not contemplate leaving the security of Park House, in Sandringham, where we were based with my father; and Althorp seemed such an old man's house, reflecting my grandfather's Edwardian tastes, in a chilling time-warp complete with the permeating smell of Trumper's hair oil and the ubiquitous tocking of grandfather clocks – their ticking always seemed too subtle a sound, getting absorbed in the oak of the floorboards and the fabric of the tapestries.

Another problem was actually getting to Althorp. It was over two hours in the car from Park House, and that was an age in my father's too-smooth Jaguar, with the result that we would reach the Park gates after several stops for car-sickness. There would then be the stately pace through the Park, as my father absorbed the magic of this most English

Althorp, home to the Spencer family for nearly 500 years.

2

of settings, where the twentieth century was not welcome and where natural beauty was the perpetual theme.

We would nudge past lambs, a reminder of my ancestors' great flocks from medieval times, ignore the turn-off to the Falconry, and cruise on to the cattle grid. There were no 'sleeping policemen' then, which made the grid that much more of a feature. And there, on the right, would be the façade of a house that had been home to nearly five centuries of Spencers, and would one day, they told me, swallow me up too. The Stables, with their mellow, yellow glow of ironstone, looked so much softer, so much more inviting – the warmth of the feminine, in contrast to the house's steely masculinity.

I have never, ever, heard anyone call the exterior of Althorp beautiful. Not even architectural historians, whom you might expect to stick up for their own, have defended it thus. The dappled grey of the external tiles emits no feeling of joy, the shallowness of their form betrayed by the drabness of their effect. How I have longed that my great-great-great-grandfather had ignored fashion and stuck with the original red-brick façade, rather than let Henry Holland impose his grey, Georgian tastes on a Tudor and Stuart gem. But the work was done; and, on a practical level, it has ensured the outward survival of Althorp, without too much maintenance, for over two centuries. The trouble is, it looks like a 'practical' solution. No romantic would ever countenance such a course.

So imagine a small boy, arriving after a long journey at the most imposing of settings, with family expectation oozing from every elderly pore of every adult relation, and you will understand part of the reason why Althorp, and its inheritance, was not something that I overly looked forward to.

It all seems very spoilt and immature now, I appreciate; but I had no idea that I would ever be able to impose my own tastes and priorities on something so historic, so very settled. For my grandfather was not known as 'the curator earl' without reason, and for him Althorp was a living conservation exercise, where he could catalogue and maintain, with enormous diligence, while sharing the collection generously with fellow members of the intelligentsia, and reluctantly with those who in no way matched his vast knowledge.

My memory of those days is of orderly druggets, dust sheets and

'Grandmother's Sitting Room'.

uniformity. My grandmother's *joie de vivre* was limited to 'Grand-mother's Sitting Room', with beautiful, deep blue, hand-painted frescoes and formal furniture that reflected her cool and natural aristocracy; a slice of sophistication in an otherwise stolidly traditional English stately home.

The last time I remember being with my grandmother was outside this room, through the french windows in her Rose Garden, her head swathed in bandages after an unsuccessful operation to root out a brain tumour, giggling as we played with her hose-pipe, neither splashing the other but threatening to, before we hugged each other tight, me breath-less with childish excitement, she knowing that there would not be too many hugs left with her grandchildren during this lifetime. She died that November.

4

One of the hand-painted frescoes in 'Grandmother's Sitting Room'.

My grandfather dominated the rest of Althorp. He combined the authority of his inherited status with the assuredness of encyclopedic knowledge. He could recite not only the creator of every piece of furniture, but also how much it cost, when and where it was repaired, as well as stating from which room in which Spencer property it had originated.

Grandfather pored over the family records in the Muniment Room – a musty apartment beyond the dinginess of his own secretary's garret, where 500 years of Spencer papers were amassed: medieval household accounts, letters from leading Jacobean political figures, and reminiscences of Victorian house parties, all stored together.

Grandfather once found Sir Winston Spencer-Churchill, busy researching for his biography of their mutual ancestor, the First Duke of Marlborough, smoking a cigar in this holy of holies, and made him douse it immediately in a glass of water. I'm not sure who would, on reflection, have been more taken aback at this: Churchill for the uncompromising abruptness of his host, or my grandfather, who would not have considered whom he was ordering about until after the immediate threat to his archives had been extinguished. As a rule, Grandfather was very conscious of people's status.

The Muniment Room is now gone, its contents with the British Library, much of it awaiting cataloguing. I doubt whether Grandfather ever thought of anything as mundane as an index; he knew his way round those family papers half instinctively and half through the accumulated experience of thousands of hours spent researching his family history, which he found a great deal more interesting than anyone or anything else on the planet.

Yet that is to take nothing away from the contribution made by Grandfather to the continuity of possession of the bulk of the contents of Althorp. He survived the swingeing taxation regimes of the 1950s to 1970s through parsimony, keeping a standard of living that he probably felt to be below that of his birthright, but single-minded in his quest to keep all his inheritance together.

There were mistakes, of course. In the 1930s, short of cash as ever and determined to finance my father's education, he sold the great Holbein of Henry VIII. In King Charles' catalogue, this masterpiece was described with relish by His Majesty's curator:

No hair is visible under the cap or beside the ears; the hairs of the beard and moustaches are very fine and thin. The eyeballs are clear blue-gray ... The sleeves of his doublet are of cloth of gold; the underdress is of lavender gray, covered with a beautiful pattern in fine lines ... The picture is painted in oil on a very solid piece of English oak.

Grandfather sold Holbein's small but perfect portrait for £10,000. To be fair, that must have seemed a fortune at the time. However, it is now the centrepiece of the Thyssen collection in Madrid, and the last time I heard it valued, several years ago, the experts were speaking in terms of $50 million. Even allowing for inflation and every other possible variable since, this was clearly not a good sale. Indeed, my father would often readily admit, with that wonderful twinkle in his eye, that his education, although solid, was perhaps slightly over-priced, when taking capital sales into account. In fact, my family often made the wrong choice when it came to selling things off; of which, more later.

But, for now, let's return to those early visits to Althorp. They were not particularly fun-filled occasions; I can clearly remember that. On arrival, Ainsley Pendrey, the butler, would open the door and be charming, always crisply turned out in his black and white, his hair smoothed back, his smile genuine. As a child, you tended to register these glimmers of happiness.

My father and grandfather had an uneasy relationship – there were no sinister reasons for this; rather, I believe, Grandfather found it hard

Edward John, later Eighth Earl Spencer, by Rodrigo Moynihan, ARA.

Albert Edward John, Seventh Earl Spencer, by Augustus John.

to accept that his custodianship of Althorp was to be limited by his own mortality, and he did not enjoy seeing his successor, in middle age, quietly awaiting his turn as master of the house. The fact that the next earl was his own flesh and blood was irrelevant: Grandfather and Althorp were so intertwined in his own psyche that anyone else entering into the relationship was an intruder.

For his part, my father was wary of Grandfather's temper, and was conscious of the fact that he would not be allowed to have any say in the dealings of Althorp until the old man had breathed his last. It was sad, particularly in the years following Grandmother's death and my parents' divorce, that these two lonely men, who both had so much to give, could not break through the distance they had established between one another, to enjoy each other as men, even if not as father and son.

I remember 'the three generations' sitting down to a lunch in the Tapestry Dining Room. It was silent, apart from the noises of my grandfather eating with great gusto, a napkin tucked in around his neck, hanging down over his popping-out tummy, and it was very sad and tense. We all missed Grandmother, who would have kept proceedings – if not the food – light; a touchstone for us all and a facilitator of

The Tapestry Dining Room.

easy relations. But her place was empty. Her peerless posture, backbone absolutely straight, was gone for ever. We were all lost without her.

The food was always indescribably bad – the epitome of overcooked English ghastliness, which was acceptable in the 70s but wouldn't be countenanced even in a prison canteen today. I know my memory isn't playing tricks when I recall with a shudder that the vegetables were boiled onions. Yes, it was that grim.

Lunch concluded with Grandfather performing his trick, which both thrilled and disgusted us, his grandchildren. He didn't like coffee, but it did have the benefit of being hot, and it could dissolve sugar, so Grandfather would ladle in heaped spoonfuls – and these were large spoons, designed to trowel into sugar bowls, rather than quarry neatly off the top – into his half-cup of weak coffee, then flick the whole, treacly contents into his mouth, crunching the undissolved crystals with huge satisfaction. In his lonely old age, his tastebuds had become his closest friends.

By this stage, I had looked at all the familiar features in this room which made it human for a small boy, rather than simply another assembly of family treasures. The two tapestries were wonderfully vivid, protected by the darkness of a room that had but one window and was replete with sombre oak panelling, brought from the original Spencer home of Wormleighton, in neighbouring Warwickshire. The panelling must have looked imposing in the Court of the Star Chamber of that mansion, the bulk of which – and it was a bulk, being four times the size of Althorp – was burnt down by Royalists in the English Civil War. But in that smallest of the house's dining rooms it just looked sombre.

The tapestries, however, with their bucolic scenes, one of gypsies and one of farming, were stimulating for a young mind, keen to distance itself from the far-too-adult tensions of the room. The blue of the jay reminded me of the birds you would often see on the approach to the Falconry at the back of the Park. The sheep and cattle were familiar beasts, of course; the goats marginally less so. But the faces of the gypsies were what entranced me, with their fresh features and their lively eyes. To me, they were real.

My reverie and lunch ended as my father and grandfather stood up. There seemed to be relief all round that the ordeal by food was over. I walked over to Grandfather, and placed my hand in his as we left the room. Unused to receiving simple, unquestioning love, the old man started to cry. I didn't notice it myself, but my father told me, many years later, with regret in his voice that this was a rare breaching of the tough veneer of a man who lost his mother at a very young age and somehow never recovered from the blow.

During our childhood my sisters and I rarely stayed the night at Althorp when my grandfather was there. If we did, it was in the Night Nursery, between the Nursery proper and Grandmother's Bedroom.

It was a terrifying house to stay in: the vastness of the place was somehow even more pronounced at night, with the sound of footsteps outside the room, and the opening and closing of doors discernible. This was the nightwatchman, doing his hourly patrols, with torch in one hand and cosh in the other. At least his presence was expected; it was the unexplained creakings of the ancient building's infrastructure that really caused alarm – especially to children terrified of the dark. Our short candles never lasted the whole night.

The nightwatchman had the least enviable job on the Estate, single-handedly watching over the treasures of Althorp between 8 p.m. and 8 a.m. The first lines of defence were the shutters on the windows, complete with bells hanging from the inside. In 1954 these were breached, Higgerson, the nightwatchman, bursting into Grandfather's room to tell him that he had seen an intruder in the South Drawing Room. Armed with his service revolver, with which he had regrettably blown his horse's ear off during cavalry manœuvres forty years earlier, Grandfather charged downstairs, loosing off a shot at the fleeing figure. Perhaps because he was neither equine, nor stationary, the thief got away unscathed, with a painted picture frame under his arm. Grandfather concluded, with the disdain he reserved for anyone who came to Althorp – criminal, guest or day-tripper – who failed to understand the worth of the house's contents, that the dimwitted intruder had probably thought the frame was gold.

Back then, and until quite recently, there was no sophisticated burglar alarm nor smoke detection system. The nightwatchmen – the first of whom I recall, Mr Ward, with his twinkly eyes, rosy cheeks, grey

The South Drawing Room.

goatee beard and thinning hair, looked like a highly animated elf – had a huge responsibility, with only their hourly call to the police as a link with the wider world.

One Christmas Eve we children went to chat to the nightwatchman in the Staff Room. I don't remember his name, but I do know that he was a very unhappy man – my father said that he had a horrendously difficult wife, which explained his choice of job – and that we quickly established that he had no Christmas presents to look forward to. We were appalled, for my father always festooned us with presents, our stockings alone being the envy of our schoolfriends. We retreated upstairs for a conference, and then reappeared with our offering – poorly wrapped 'whimsies', animal figurines that we both collected. It was the only time I ever saw that particular nightwatchman smile.

Before the nightwatchman, there was a night porter on constant duty through the night; more servant than security officer. The hall porter's chair from Spencer House, the family's London seat, can still be seen in the main entrance hall at Althorp. It's a wonderfully comfortable piece of furniture, with padded red leather, no doubt so the hall porter could doze, while being in an almost-ready state if summoned in the darkness hours.

This room is known as the Wootton Hall, so-called because of the huge canvases on the walls, painted by the early eighteenth-century artist, John Wootton, employed by a former Charles Spencer, then owner of Althorp, to capture his patron's love of equestrian sports, particularly fox-hunting. All the local squirearchy are captured, but so also are the other components of the hunt – the kennel men, the grooms, even the terriers and earth-stoppers. I love the way the pictures cross-refer: the prime characters from the portraits becoming bit-part men, expert in their roles, in the bigger pictures. We even have the hunting horn from one of the paintings sitting today on the hall porter's chair.

Wootton painted all these works in 1733, in his studio in Marylebone, London, before they were transported to their permanent home at Althorp. According to the diary of the First Earl of Egremont, when he saw these works for the first time before they were actually dispatched to Charles Spencer, they fully confirmed Wootton to be 'the best painter of horses in England'. Certainly they make for an impressive welcome to the house, in the perfectly proportioned hall, two storeys high. Sir Nikolaus Pevsner, the great architectural historian, rated this 'the noblest Georgian room in the county' of Northamptonshire.

For a room that has such elegance, with its made-to-measure paintings, it has a varied history, with an assortment of objects covering the eighteenth to twentieth centuries. This is typical of Althorp, for it has changed appearance regularly, both inside and out, since my family

The Wootton Hall, the striking Palladian entrance to Althorp.

moved there in 1508. It has also been the most consistently inhabited of several houses owned by my family over the generations, and has ended up this century as the final repository of the cream of the Spencer family's chattels.

A detail from one of the mahogany hall chairs, decorated with the family coat of arms.

It is not only the hall porter's chair whose provenance is Spencer House. The handsome hall chairs – a set of a dozen – are not upholstered, since the family's visitors would have braved all types of weather on their journey on horseback, and there was no point in having quality fabric ruined by damp or muddy coats. They are my favourite pieces of furniture in the house, the griffin from the family coat of arms painted boldly on their backs against a cool grey-blue background.

Then there is the sedan chair, rediscovered in the Stable Block in 1911, but originally from Spencer House; the Countess's transport through the squalor of London's streets in the eighteenth century.

Behind you as you enter is a pair of marble statues of 'blackamoors', images of captured slaves to some Roman household, discovered in the silt of the River Tiber, and given to the First Duke of Marlborough by his brother – and brother-in-arms – General Charles Churchill. Apart from lacking the bows they should clearly be holding, they are in extraordinarily fine condition, the marble almost unblemished, their quivers by their sides still full. For such classical works, they have a remarkably relaxed air, almost modern in stance and expression.

Above them hang various flags. The one that used to capture my imagination as a boy was the White Ensign from the motor torpedo boat commanded by my hero, Cecil Spencer, my great-uncle. I had always been interested in him because we shared a birthday, fellow Taureans. Beyond that coincidence, his derring-do was thrilling to a little boy – great-nephew or not.

He had drawn the Germans' fire from the main strike force when Admiral Roger John Brownlow Keyes took Zeebrugge for the British in 1918. A copy of the Admiral's commendation at Uncle Cecil's courage explains why he ended the Great War with two Distinguished Service

One of the pair of Italian black and Breschia marble blackamoor torchères.

The ceiling of the Wootton Hall with its plaster flowers – each one different.

Crosses, the Croix de Guerre and a reputation for bravery that makes his eventual death, falling off a horse on Malta, tragically mundane.

The extraordinary quality this room has is in *demanding* that your eye roves round it, exploring all its attributes. Particularly striking are the plaster flowers on the ceiling, the work of Colen Campbell, one of the greatest architects of the early eighteenth century. As a tour guide twenty-odd years ago, I used to notice that, as soon as I had revealed that each of the dozens of flowers was of a unique design, the visitors would take the comment as a challenge, straining to spot two that were identical. They tried in vain to find a flaw in Campbell's artful design.

And then there is the Wootton Hall floor, which looks as though it is part of the original sophisticated design. In fact, the black and white checked marble was a twentieth-century addition, part of the subtle remodelling performed, with the most limited of budgets, by my great-grandfather, Robert, when he became earl in 1910.

Robert had used this room for the lying in state of his half-brother, the Red Earl, so the surrounding population could pay their respects to

'The Red Earl', John Poyntz, Fifth Earl Spencer, lying in state in the Wootton Hall.

the venerable old man of the county, who had been Lord Lieutenant of Ireland and Gladstone's choice as his successor as Prime Minister. Photographs show the Red Earl, his beard no longer dramatically red but shot through with grey, his proud face restful above his Knight of the Garter robes.

Until the middle of the nineteenth century the floor was of simple stone, a reminder that this was not always an enclosed room, but the archway to the central courtyard of the original, Tudor house. Robert's black and white marble replaced the piecemeal repairs of his father, Frederick, the Fourth Earl, who had put down brown and blue tiles. It is hard to see how that colour scheme could have worked in such a space. The 1910 switch to marble finally put a line through any link with the days when horse and carriage arrived inside, as opposed to in front of, Althorp.

Although nobody knows when the first house stood in its present position, essential repair work to the front wall of the Wootton Hall in the 1950s revealed medieval windows, which seemed to the workmen and experts of the time to predate the 1508 structure that was my ancestors' first home here. There would have been nothing strange about building over a prior structure: a good site was a good site after all, and why waste materials?

Initially my family was interested in Althorp for the grazing, rather than because it might provide a suitable second home to Worm-leighton. In 1486 they were nearing the peak of their skill at rearing huge flocks of sheep, and land accumulation was a natural con-sequence of their success. At first they were only able to lease the land that now constitutes the bulk of the Park from the Catesby family, Northamptonshire and Warwickshire squires, one of whose number was a major protagonist of the ill-fated Gunpowder Plot in 1605.

But in 1508 Althorp was bought by John Spencer for £800, and the house that you see today had its heart constructed as the family's Northamptonshire base. It took only four years for the new occupants to create a park, initially comprising 300 acres of grassland, 100 acres of woodland, and 40 acres of water. At that stage it was called 'Oldthorpe'. Prior to that, in the Domesday Book of 1087, it had been catalogued as 'Olletorp', which meant 'Olla's Thorp'. My father told me that Olla was a Saxon lord. In the thirteenth and fifteenth centuries respectively, it was recorded as 'Holtropp' and 'Aldrop'. The ancient roots of the name explain the reason why 'Althorp' is pronounced 'Awltrupp', rather than as it would appear on paper; for 'thorp' is a Scandinavian word, which would have been pronounced as 'throop', or perhaps 'thrupp'. From the Danish, it would have been most accurately translated as meaning 'daughter settlement'.

During my childhood I never heard any of my family refer to the

Edward John, Eighth Earl Spencer, in the drive at Althorp.

place as 'All-thorp'. My grandfather only ever called it 'Awl-trupp', as did all his generation. My father resigned himself to the wrong pronunciation, because he was fed up with correcting those who, understandably, did not know the traditional one. He would also say with a smile that it helped people find it on the map, which might encourage day-trippers to come and spend money in Raine's gift shop.

When I inherited the place in 1992, the BBC Pronunciation Department sent me a letter, stating their hope that I would revert to the correct pronunciation, and giving me strict guidelines on what this should be. I assured them that I did not know it as anything else, and would therefore do so. I felt slightly let down then, at the time of my late sister's funeral, when the BBC agreed with their ITV rivals to go for 'All-thorp'. Even more so when it was later reported to me that an American television correspondent describing the final moments of that tragic ceremony at Westminster Abbey, when my youngest sister's funeral took place, concluded with: 'The coffin will now go to its final resting place, at Antwerp.' Diana would have enjoyed that.

Eventually you come to terms with the fact that people call the place what they want; so long as they respect and accept its history, which is for the most part unequivocal.

The original John Spencer – there were many more, since pretty much every eldest son since has been endowed with this most English of first names – was an accumulator: when he acquired Althorp, he also became lord of the manor of Fenny Compton, in Warwickshire, Stoneton, Nobottle, Great Brington, Little Brington, Harlestone, Glassthorpe, Flore, Wicken, Wyke Hamon, Upper Boddington, Lower Boddington and Hinton. There were also land acquisitions in Badby, Daventry, Barby, Guilsborough, East Haddon, Holdenby, Brockhall, Hanging Houghton and Church Brampton.

The previous year, 1507, John had secured the lordship of Wormleighton from the Cope family, and started to build the manor house for himself and sixty of his relatives. I have a sneaking suspicion that my early sixteenth-century ancestors must have struck their Northamptonshire and Warwickshire neighbours as appallingly voracious in their acquisitions, and more than a little *nouveau riche* in the way they threw their money about. The neighbours were probably correct, except on one count: this was not the willy-nilly scattering of money it may have appeared to be, but the considered accumulation of some of the finest grazing land in England. Direct connections with over half these acquisitions survive today.

The original John Spencer became known in family circles as 'the Founder'. We know of little that happened to Althorp in the immediate aftermath of his scatter-gun buying. It seems probable that the new house in Northamptonshire enjoyed a fair amount of family occupation; a fact borne out by the Founder's son's will, which 'ordered hospitality to be kept in his houses at Althorp, &c., by his heir, after his decease, according as he had done'. We also know that it was a moated house, being built within living memory of the discord of the Wars of the Roses, so the moat would have been decorative but with defensive undertones.

The confidence of the sixteenth-century Spencers that they were in this part of Northamptonshire to stay is demonstrated by the planting of oak trees in the Park. In my early teens I used to come across stone tablets throughout the property. The Founder's grandson was the first to leave his mark in this way. You can still read, carved on a tablet:

'This Wood was Planted by
Sir John Spencer Knight
Grandfather of Robert Lord
Spencer in the Yearers of
our Lord 1567 and 1568.'

A similar memorial in near-by woodland states:

'This Wood was Planted by
Sir John Spencer Knight
Father of Robert Lord
Spencer in the yeare
of our Lord 1589.'

The latter is in 'Sir John's Wood', a corner of the Park between the old kennels and the outskirts of Great Brington. The year of this planting is perhaps its most significant feature, since it was the one immediately following the destruction of the Spanish Armada. My father said that, nervous of further invasion fleets from Philip II, many magnates planted trees to provide timber for the construction of a stronger English

The Picture Gallery, 115 feet of oak passageway hung with a superb collection of portraits.

naval force. Four centuries on these plantations have been spared active duty, and are now reaching the end of their non-combatant lives. It is amazing to think that they have seen everything that has gone on in Althorp Park through succeeding generations. Indeed, since the house has been subject to major transformations during each century of its existence, they are almost the purest reminders of the original tastes and aspirations of the Founder and his sixteenth-century successors.

I say 'almost' because one room in Althorp is as it was when the first structure was erected by my family: the Picture Gallery.

I love the Picture Gallery. As a tour guide, I would show the visitors round the ground floor of the house, with its contents well ordered but conventional: chairs by the fireplace, bookcases against the wall, side-tables where you would expect them. The only surprises for those unfamiliar with the place lay in the variety of the objects and the sheer number of paintings on the walls.

The Picture Gallery then offers a complete change of pace – almost a change of venue, as the Georgian influences are thrown back and the starkness of the original Tudor roots of the place are laid bare. I defy anybody to walk into that room and not catch their breath: it is designed to provoke that reaction. For this is 115 feet of oak passageway, 20 feet wide and 19 high. It is like looking down a kaleidoscope, with glittering images all the way along the sides, but with the brightest of all at the end.

You have to have a pretty striking painting to bring people's attention to a focal point over 100 feet away, when there is so much to distract them on either side. Over the centuries many pictures have left my family's ownership. Thankfully, Van Dyck's *War and Peace* remains.

It was never actually bought by any of my ancestors, but was a gift from an in-law. It shows George Digby, Second Earl of Bristol, and William, First Duke of Bedford, both standing in noble arrogance, brothers-in-law and aristocrats; the full-length epitome of self-assuredness and male beauty. Marchioness Grey, a visitor to the Picture Gallery in 1748, summed it up best in a letter to a friend: 'Indeed there is a gracefulness and life in the figures beyond what I ever saw, they are quite animated and a strength of colouring that strikes you from one end of that gallery to the other. It is so beautiful that a picture which hangs by it is hurt by its situation.' It is the quintessential 'swagger portrait'.

The painting has become known as *War and Peace* because of the way the two men have been placed in their respective contexts: the Duke is the dominant figure, in bright red, with silver lace, a breastplate in front of him and a helmet behind; and behind is Digby, in less dashing black satin and laced ruff, surrounded by symbols of learning and culture, the satellites of peace. It has always been my favourite painting in the house, because of its sense of drama. Forget the 'Peace' aspect of the double portrait: to me as a boy, these men encapsulated what I then saw as the glamour of warfare – in particular, of the English Civil War, which I took to be about thundering cavalry charges behind Prince Rupert of the Rhine, when passion and gallantry seemed more seductive than the relentless professional discipline of the opposing Parliamentarians.

My grandfather was so concerned that this painting should never be exposed to destruction in a fire that he had the nearest tall window in the Gallery turned into a huge door-like structure with hinges down one side, so that the whole frame could be lifted off the wall and lowered down to safety outside. My father, who sold a fair proportion of the finer objects in the house, once promised me that he would never allow *War and Peace* to join the seemingly endless exodus to Bond Street salerooms. It has an almost sacred place at the heart of the collection, being at once the most valuable item in the house and the most striking. To many it is one of the greatest Van Dycks still in private ownership, and I am proud that it remains at Althorp.

But this is just the centrepiece of a room laden with glories; one that has long been recognized as something out of the ordinary. In 1760 Horace Walpole wrote: 'Althorpe [*sic*] has several very fine pictures by the best Italian hands, and a gallery of all one's acquaintances by Vandyke [*sic*] and Lely.' He went on to boast, 'In the gallery I found myself quite at home; and surprised the housekeeper by my familiarity with the portraits.' I imagine the housekeeper was only too pleased to see the back of him.

Indeed, it would have been surprising if the Picture Gallery's subject matter had not been familiar to any man of learning. There are portraits of James I, looking dour and unattractive, his natural shyness betrayed by the hostility with which he seems to greet the onlooker. Whenever I look at this portrait, I think of James's exasperation at his

War and Peace by Sir Anthony Van Dyck.

James I, after Jan de Critz.

advisers' insistence that he show himself more to his people, to rival the way in which his predecessor, Elizabeth I, had so successfully played the public relations game. 'God's wounds!' he finally exploded. 'And would they also see my arse?' The anger and the coarseness of the first king of Scotland and England are there, clearly visible, in the Picture Gallery at Althorp.

Charles II, on the other hand, looks smugly down on the Gallery, as well he might, since a dozen of the paintings there, by his court artist, Sir Peter Lely, comprise a collection that has come to be known as the

Charles II, by Mary Beale.

'Windsor Beauties'. These are Charles's principal mistresses. Heavy-bosomed, with ringleted hair, they are not obviously beautiful by modern standards, but they have a sexiness, an air of confidence in their own desirability, that doubtless explains their popularity with their monarch.

At the time of Walpole's remarks, the portrait of another monarch was also in the Picture Gallery: Lady Jane Grey, 'The Nine Days' Queen', painted by Lucas de Heere. It is still at Althorp, though in a different room now, and shows Lady Jane aged sixteen, a year before

Lady Jane Grey, by Lucas de Heere.

her execution, sitting in a room at Broadgate, her father's family home in Leicestershire, reading a religious text, pretty in a red velvet dress. It is poignant to see the devotion to Protestantism of this young girl, a devotion that was to lose her her head when the Catholics overthrew her, the sincere and innocent pawn of power-broking lords.

As you look today at the sheer handsomeness of this room, with its panelling along the walls and its wide wooden floorboards, you feel the history of the house at its rawest. Tudor ladies liked to use the length of the gallery for exercise, walking up and down it on wet days, in order to spare their long skirts and dresses from being dragged through the mud outside. There would have been little in the way of furniture in such a space. However, generations previous to ours were much more flexible in their use of the rooms, so we hear one eighteenth-century female house guest recalling the Picture Gallery as being 'a fine room for walking about in – we always breakfast there'.

Indeed, in 1695 the neighbouring nobility and gentry gathered to dine there. They had come to pay their respects to William III, as he in turn had come to secure the support of Robert Spencer, Second Earl of Sunderland and master of Althorp, one of the least trusted, but most influential, politicians of his time. To quote from Thomas Macaulay's *History of England*:

It seems strange that he [William] should, in the course of what was really a canvassing tour, have honoured with such a mark of favour a man so generally distrusted and hated as Sunderland. But the people were determined to be pleased. All Northamptonshire crowded to kiss that royal hand in that fine gallery which had been embellished by the pencil of Vandyck and made classic by the muse of Waller, and the Earl tried to conciliate his neighbours by feasting them at eight tables, all blazing with plate.

Two hundred and ninety-nine years later I gave a dinner party in the same room. The occasion was not a royal visit nor a political exercise, but the rather more humdrum business of my thirtieth birthday. There was one table, with 128 people seated round it, allowing this often neglected section of the house to come alive for an evening; a faint echo of past glories, but I hope enjoyable enough. Since the kitchens were 300 yards away, the food was pretty average – shades of Grandfather's time! – but the sight of the room 'blazing with plate' once more was something I will never forget.

In the Picture Gallery, between the 'Windsor Beauties' and *War and Peace*, is a tiny door cut neatly into the oak panelling. It is almost never used and leads to a modest staircase that joins the Pink Suite, a guest bedroom, to the rest of the house. My great-aunt, Margaret Douglas-Home, was the youngest of six children who lived at Althorp from 1910 onwards. She was Grandfather's baby sister, and she lived a solitary existence, mainly with the servants, because her mother had haemorrhaged to death within hours of Margaret's birth. Family folklore has it that Margaret's father Robert, Sixth Earl Spencer, who was famously in love with his wife, never fully forgave his youngest child for the part she had unwittingly played in leaving him an inconsolable widower.

This quasi-exile from the rest of the family must have been very hurtful to a young girl of great sensitivity and insight. However, Aunt Margaret, who outlived all her siblings by over a decade, was never one to feel sorry for herself, and she threw herself into living in such a huge house with enormous enthusiasm. I used to visit her in her tiny cottage in Norfolk, and listen in awe as this highly entertaining, deeply intelligent lady recalled snippets from her childhood.

'And, of course, there was the girl in grey slippers,' she suddenly volunteered one day, after a moment's involuntary rasping due to emphysema.

'What girl with grey slippers?' I asked.

'Oh, haven't I told you about my friend? She lived in the Picture Gallery, by the little door. I never told anyone at the time, because I knew they would just say, "Oh, Margaret!" and roll their eyes at me. But she was there, all right. I used to spend hours with her, just talking. She was so small, so fine looking, with the most beautiful grey satin slippers. When we had finished, she would just drift away, through the door.'

'And what would you talk about?' I prompted, half-cynic, half-believer.

'Well, that's the curious part. I never could recall what we said to one another. We would just talk, and as soon as the conversation was concluded, I would not remember a word we had said. It didn't bother me; no, not at all. What was said wasn't important; the fact that we *played* together was the important part.'

It is easy to dismiss this tale as the musings of a confused octogenarian, nearing the end of her life. But Aunt Margaret was remarkably lucid until her final months, recalling with the most extraordinary detail events from her earliest years – ranging from George V's Coronation to her more bizarre relations' visits to Althorp – and I feel that she genuinely believed she had had these games with her anonymous friend, whose footwear was more memorable than any other feature. Whether the girl was in fact imaginary, ghostly or whatever, for me the little door will always be the home of 'the girl with the grey slippers'.

I have never seen a ghost; not at Althorp, nor elsewhere. People who believe in them will be relieved to know that many other people claim to have done so. The nearest I have ever got to being personally involved in a sighting was in 1994, when I had friends staying for a weekend in the summer.

The day before the guests arrived I had been thumbing through some leather-bound volumes relating to the house. One of these was a book of press-cuttings from the mid nineteenth century kept by my great-great-grandfather, Frederick, Fourth Earl Spencer. In it was a curious story about a house party at Althorp, attended by, among others, the Dean of Lincoln.

One morning, so the article said, the Dean came down to breakfast with the family and rather frostily complained to the then earl that in future he would prefer it if he was left undisturbed after retiring for the night. My ancestor asked the Dean to expand. It transpired that the Dean had been awoken by a figure dressed as a groom entering his room, holding candles, who had gone round the bed, checking all the candles were properly snuffed out.

Apparently, there was silence from my family. They then asked for an exact description of the 'groom'. After this was given, they all agreed that it was the ghost of the previous earl's favourite servant – indeed, a groom – whose job it was to go round all the rooms at night, after every-one had retired, to check that no naked flame was still burning.

The day I read this, I thought nothing more of it. I closed the book, which I had never opened before, and put it back in the bookshelf, an anonymous red spine in several shelves of similar volumes.

On the Sunday evening, I was helping my guests down with their luggage from the same room, the Oak Bedroom, when the girl of the couple said, 'Do you know, I swear that someone came in here last night.' I did not pay much attention at first, because I thought it could

The Oak Bedroom, where the secret marriage of the First Earl took place.

have been someone going to bed late, who had had trouble finding their own room.

'And the strange thing is, he was holding a candelabrum and wearing an old uniform – a cloak.' Well, I have a broad range of guests at Althorp, but none eccentric enough to dress up like that. 'Hang on a minute.' I said, and ran up to where Joyce, the housekeeper, was cataloguing articles for a new museum she had created, showing off some of the more curious historic items that had previously been confined to storage rooms. I was about to bring down a groom's cloak, when I hesitated, and reached instead for a footman's uniform. If she's fibbing, I thought, this'll catch her out. I then raced back downstairs again, and showed the clothing to my guest. 'Almost . . .', she said, 'but it was longer – more like this . . .' And she described in detail the apparel of an early nineteenth-century Spencer groom.

The overriding association my family has with the Oak Bedroom is not, however, of the ghostly, but rather of the romantic kind. It was here that John Spencer, later the First Earl, married his sweetheart in secret. It is a story worth exploring in some detail, as it reveals how

Georgiana Poyntz, wife of the First Earl Spencer, by Pompeo Batoni.

34

the house was enjoyed in the mid eighteenth century, when the family's money must have seemed limitless, and its status was consequently at its peak.

This John Spencer was the eldest son of another John, who in turn was the favourite grandson of the original Duchess of Marlborough. Sarah Marlborough had a fortune so vast that she actually lent money to the Bank of England. This financial clout, the irascible old matriarch was determined, was not to go to her senior grandson, the Third Duke of Marlborough, but to his younger brother, John, known as Jack – a reprobate, in all honesty, who died young through what was politely termed 'excess'. Horace Walpole was slightly more incisive in pinpointing the main causes of Jack's early demise, when writing to Sir Horace Mann in 1746: 'Jack Spencer, old Marlborough's Grandson and heir, is just dead, at the age of six or seven and thirty, and in possession of near £30,000 a year, merely because he would not be abridged of these invaluable blessings of an English subject, brandy, small beer, and tobacco.'

The twelve-year-old John was left beneficiary to the greatest inheritance in the kingdom. A delicate youth, he certainly did not shirk from enjoying his fortune, spending it on diamond-buckled shoes, vast retinues of retainers, and, latterly, on building Spencer House, overlooking London's Green Park, as well as indulging in the fiercely competitive and heinously expensive business of fighting elections to Parliament – which effectively meant bribing people to vote for his candidate rather than that of another magnate. One such campaign alone was to cost him £120,000, ruining two opposing peers in the process.

The only pressure on a young man of this scale of wealth was to marry, in order to ensure the money stayed in the direct family line rather than being syphoned off to cadet branches. By 1755, as John's twenty-first birthday approached, it became evident that Georgiana Poyntz was to be the chosen one. She was no great heiress, but the groom's financial position made that consideration irrelevant. This was a genuine love match, certainly judging by the breathy letters Georgiana wrote to her friends about her man, 'handsomer than an angel': 'I will own it, and never deny it again, that I do love Spencer above all men upon earth.' She passed the test of staying at Althorp

John, First Earl Spencer, by Sir Thomas Gainsborough.

that summer, reporting back that, 'I never saw anything so charming as the Park here.' She was also tolerant of the quirkiness of the house.

John Spencer's idea of fun for his guests varied from the quite sophisticated to the basic. Georgiana was so in love that it all seemed wonderful. Beside the water of the Round Oval, where her great-great-great-great-granddaughter was to be buried two and a half centuries later, the house party dined under a large tree, which was garlanded with flowers by the gardeners. Musicians played French horns from the other side of the water, screened from the view of the diners.

Slightly less restful, and much more distracting, must have been the noise of a dozen small hounds, who were let off their leads in order to chase round and round the many hares that lived in this part of the Park. 'I do not know whether you are fond of the cry of hounds,' Georgiana rather unconvincingly wrote to a friend, 'but to me there is nothing so charming.'

One of the house guests, Lord Fordwick, celebrated his birthday during this stay, so there was, of all things, a donkey race in the grounds of Althorp. Only the men could enter, and the winner was to be the man whose donkey came last. The twist lay in the fact that nobody was to ride their own donkey: all the riders therefore had to attempt to get the donkey they rode to the finishing line first, while discouraging the one they actually owned from completing the course before the others.

Local villagers were brought in during the evening for a dancing contest. A guinea was the prize for the best dancer, the sole judge being John's mother. No doubt the rich prize made the condescension of the exercise more palatable to the participants.

The following day it was back to the hearty, knockabout pastimes, and the 'sack race' was performed with fifty competitors. More than thirty of them fell immediately and failed to get up again, so tightly tied were the sacks. However, mindful of the first prize of thirty shillings, many of the local competitors had been practising their sack-racing. Some, Georgiana noted, could 'go as fast as anybody can walk'. In the end John gave everyone two shillings for turning up, while not stinting on the top prize money.

Having not only survived what appears to have amounted almost to a Hooray Henry Olympics, but having actually enjoyed it as well, Georgiana was soon in possession of an engagement ring. There was a ruby in the centre of it, surrounded by diamonds, which in turn were encircled by further, smaller, rubies. Two mottoes were written on the ring: the first, for public consumption, read, '*Mon coeur est tout à toi*; the other – hidden – Georgiana never showed to anyone, and read, *Gardez le tien pour moi*.

It was decided the wedding would take place after the celebrations at Althorp of John's coming of age, scheduled for the week leading up to and including Christmas 1755. And so it was that in mid-December, twelve miles short of the Estate, they were greeted by the mayor and all the tradesmen of Northampton, who accompanied the couple and their own retinue through the town, one hundred horsemen in front, the coaches of family members in the middle and a small army of servants behind.

Two days were spent at Althorp recovering from the journey, before the couple went up to the village of Brington to inspect progress in the planning of the celebrations for the local people. A shed had been built for the occasion on the village green, with a larder and a cellar near by. Next to the temporary buildings was a huge chimney where oxen would be roasted.

Back at Althorp, the house was buzzing with activity. Cooks had been brought over from France, and the Confectioner's Room, in what is now the back yard, was churning out delicacies for the week of partying that was about to get under way.

Nothing was on a small scale, though on the Thursday night the celebrations started relatively gently, with guests having the choice of card-playing in one room, dancing in another, or listening to a concert in a third. At midnight, as soon as John Spencer's birthday had officially begun, Georgiana noted that all the bells for seven miles around started ringing. At the same time, an ox 'was laid down to roast'.

The following morning Georgiana put on a pink and silver negligée, before sitting in her dressing room with her future husband as all the house guests trooped in to pay their respects and wish them both future happiness together. All this, with music constantly coming from the hall, the excitement mounting.

John Spencer had to rush off to Brington again after breakfast, since 5,000 people had gathered there and let it be known that if Mr Spencer did not come to them in the village, they would come to him at the big house. After his arrival, they consumed over 11,000 pints of strong beer, dispersing at four, then reconvening the following day, to drink the same and eat eight oxen. Such hospitality was not so much requested of the rich young nobleman, but rather demanded by the mob.

The atmosphere was initially rather more rarified in the mansion, where Georgiana donned 'my new blue silver gown and petty coat, the Diamond cap, Pompon, necklace, earrings, and Roses for my stomacher and sleeveknots, and Nosegay'. After a reception in three rooms downstairs, the 400 diners went up to the Picture Gallery, one hundred to a table, where the French chefs showed off their artistry. 'The dinner was very fine – there were three courses, and an excessive fine dessert'; the confectioners' hard work had not been wasted.

It was then time for the gentlemen of the party to emulate their beery counterparts in Brington, as the drinking of healths concluded the dinner, each man knocking back the contents of his goblet in one. Georgiana's health was drunk three times in this way, her intended husband's once. It must have been some kickstart to the ball which ensued; the dancing led by the young and glittering couple. Georgiana records that the initial minuet was followed by a country dance. Her clothes were too heavy for dancing for long, though, so she went off to the two rooms reserved for cards. Later in life, her penchant for gambling was to lead to problems. This evening, though, it must all have seemed such innocent fun, with one room serving tea, the other cake and lemonade.

The kitchen would probably have been a scene of total chaos, as we next learn that the guests had a further supper at midnight, the 'dessert' again getting a positive mention in dispatches. Three hours later everyone collapsed. There was not enough room in Althorp for all the guests to be accommodated properly.

Unsurprisingly, Georgiana reported the following day, 'This morning my head aches a little.' She made it known that she would not be down for breakfast. It was not only reaction to the previous night's excesses that stopped her joining the other guests, but also the excitement that her marriage licence was, in all secrecy, due to arrive that day: John and Georgiana had planned to marry at Althorp on Christmas Day, with nobody else in the know.

But there was to be no stopping the mounting romanticism of John Spencer. That evening, 20 December 1755, he asked to speak to Georgiana in private. He produced the marriage licence, and then, smiling, suggested they wait no longer: would she marry him right now, in the house? He may have been half-joking, but his mother, apparently eavesdropping on the conversation, ventured that this was a wonderful idea. The wedding was on.

John's mother made the couple commence the dancing again, to avoid suspicion as to what was planned. Then, one by one, the wedding party peeled off from the ball, and convened in the Oak Bedroom, which was being occupied by John's mother and stepfather. Apart from the latter and the bride and groom, those present were Georgiana's own mother, her brother and Mr Holloway, who was not only John's tutor, but also, conveniently, a priest. It was Holloway who conducted the brief service. The bride's memory of the ceremony was straightforward: 'We both behaved very well, spoke distinct and loud, but I trembled so much I could hardly stand.' Afterwards, the group left the Oak Bedroom and rejoined the others as though nothing had happened. In this clandestine manner began a marriage that was to be famously happy.

Spencer House, London *c.* 1760, English School.
Looking across Green Park towards Buckingham House on the right.

The events of late 1755 marked a watershed in Althorp's history. Mr and Mrs John Spencer – First Earl and Countess within a decade – spent an increasing amount of time in London, especially after Spencer House was completed in 1760. There were also the distractions of the other properties, including a mansion at Wimbledon, whose park John was expanding with the aid of the great landscape designer, 'Capability' Brown, and North Creake, in Norfolk, used for shooting. John's health continued to be a worry, which resulted in his travelling to southern Europe annually to escape the worst of the English winter. Although we hear references to 'improvements' at Althorp during this period, they were as nothing to what occurred both earlier and later in the eighteenth century.

It was fortunately not uncommon for gentlemen in the seventeenth to nineteenth centuries to keep a journal of their travels, so we do have diverse accounts of Althorp throughout that period. The most evocative of the earlier ones comes from one of the household of Cosmo III of Tuscany, who paid a visit to the house in 1669, in the reign of Charles II. By this stage, the original inner courtyard had been covered over, and the magnificent staircase, still the main feature of the Saloon, had been installed.

By the time of Cosmo's visit, the house had clearly already become unrecognizable from the original Tudor red-brick manor house. As Cosmo's companion observed:

The whole of the edifice is regularly built, both as to its exterior and interior, and is richly ornamented with stone of a white colour, worked in the most exquisite manner, which is dug from a quarry at Weldon, 14 miles distant. If they could take off a certain natural roughness from this stone, and give it a polish, it would not be inferior to marble. The ascent from the ground floor to the noble storey above, is by a spacious staircase of the wood of the

walnut-tree, stained, constructed with great magnificence; this staircase, dividing itself into two equal branches, leads to the grand saloon, from which the passage into the chambers, all of them regularly disposed after the Italian manner, to which country the Earl was indebted for a model of the design, and it may be said to be the best arranged countryseat in the Kingdom; for though there may be many which surpass it in size, none are superior to it in symmetrical elegance.

The symmetry may have been lost in the intervening years, as various additions have been made, but the rest of the description will be familiar to those who know Althorp.

Six years later, the great diarist John Evelyn visited, and observed:

I went to see my Lord Sunderland's seat at Althorpe [*sic*] four miles from the ragged town of Northampton ... The house, a kind of modern building, of freestone, within most nobly furnished; the apartments very commodious, a gallery and noble hall; but the kitchen being in the body of the house, and chapel too small, were defects.

Evelyn was more generous in his appraisal of the place on a return visit in 1688:

The house, or rather palace, at Althorpe [*sic*] is a noble uniform pile in form of a half H, built of brick and freestone 'a la moderne'; the hall is well, the staircase excellent; the rooms of state, galleries, offices, and furniture, such as may become a great prince. It is situate in the midst of a garden, exquisitely planted and kept and all this in a park walled in with hewn stone, planted with rows and walks of trees, canals and fishponds and stored with game.

All these accounts relate to the time of Robert Spencer, Second Earl of Sunderland, who was Secretary of State during this period to Charles II, James II and William III. But it is as a connoisseur as opposed to a politician that we need to look at him, for he made his greatest contribution to Althorp by what he placed inside it, rather than by his Italian remodelling of the structure itself. As a young man he had embarked on the 'Grand Tour', travelling round Europe imbibing classical culture. It had the required effect, turning him into a discerning and highly knowledgeable collector. Ambassadorial stints in Paris and Madrid sharpened Robert's desire to acquire, and many of the

The Saloon with its imposing staircase, which was added in 1662, when the courtyard was enclosed.

One of a pair of paintings by Carlo Maratta showing Robert,
Second Earl of Sunderland, in classical attire on the Grand Tour.

greatest treasures of Althorp were bought by him. Two of the best of these are, in fact, full-length portraits of Robert and his companion, the Earl of Roscommon, in 'a loose drapery like an apostle', on the Grand Tour, painted by Carlo Maratti in Rome.

The most magical painting to come to Althorp during Robert's tenure – the most valuable being the Picture Gallery's *War and Peace*, via his wife, Lady Anne Digby – was by Gottfried Schalcken, whom he supposedly employed in the house. I remember it clearly as a boy.

Boy Blowing on a Fire Brand by Gottfried Schalcken.

Schalcken's particular gift was in capturing the effect of light, and this painting of a boy blowing on a firebrand, his face illuminated in a rich reflective glow, was magical in every detail. John Elsum, on seeing the picture, penned the following epigram:

> Striving to blow the brand into a flame,
> He brightens his own face and th'author's fame.

Sadly, this masterpiece was a casualty of the selling spree that followed Grandfather's time. It probably sounds pompous, but I only hope the present owner gets the joy from it that generations of my family have done.

It was Robert's desire to show his pictures off to greatest effect that spared the Picture Gallery from reshaping; although he did repanel the room with oak in 1682. Also out of a wish to preserve the paintings, and stop the mildew that used annually to attack them, he filled in the moat, planting it with flowers – 'turfed with a beautiful carpet', as the diarist John Evelyn approvingly recorded – and putting in four sets of stone steps; another deathly blow to the original Tudor form of Althorp.

Robert's involvement with his art collection went beyond that of the usual rich dilettante. He was not interested merely in having talking-points with which to impress visitors, but had a genuine commitment to the art of collecting great works. This explains why he invented his own 'Sunderland Frame', a Spanish-inspired ornate design that is the dominant one at Althorp today; the majority of the Picture Gallery's exhibits are encased in Robert's frames. They perfectly suit the portraits, adding a rich swathing to the formal poses of the subjects themselves, while lending them a gilded grandeur and softening the overall effect of the compositions.

Robert's tenure of Althorp is remarkable for one other fact: on the morning of 7 October 1693 an earthquake sent a shockwave through the Park, prompting a letter to John Evelyn from the Earl on this most un-English of phenomena.

It would be fair to say that Robert's contribution to the present collection at Althorp is second only to that of Sarah Churchill, Duchess of Marlborough; and that inheritance was secured by the second marriage of Robert's son, Charles Spencer, Third Earl of Sunderland, to Lady Anne Churchill, the Duchess of Marlborough's second, and favourite, daughter. Both the Marlboroughs' sons predeceased their father. The eldest daughter also failed to produce a male heir, so the Spencer and Churchill inheritances were now destined for one family, the Spencers.

Before this confluence of riches, Charles Spencer made his own plans for Althorp, which he held for twenty years till 1722. Like his father, he was a powerful politician who straddled reigns with skill, being one of the Principal Secretaries of State in the reigns of Queen Anne and King George I. We are interested in him here as custodian and connoisseur, not as statesman; although Althorp was recognized in his time as a bastion of Whig politics. Charles's great passion was collecting books, which he mainly did at Sunderland House in Piccadilly. The bulk of this library never came to Althorp, but later went to Blenheim Palace. However, there are records of him forming an impressive enough library at Althorp, upstairs in the Great Room.

It is easy to imagine that Charles believed Althorp, although adequate for his sheep-farming ancestors, did not quite reflect his status as the second generation of all-powerful politicians in the family. This would explain Daniel Defoe's comments, in his *Tour through Great Britain*, of 1725, that

The Earl of Sunderland's House at Althorp on the other hand has within these few years changed its face to the other extreme and had the late Earl [Charles] lived to make some new apartments, which, as we are told, were designed as two large wings to the Buildings, it would have been one of the most magnificent Palaces in Europe.

As it was, contemporaries were impressed with Charles's improvements, both in the Park and the mansion. In *A Journey through England*, an anonymous gentleman-traveller's reminiscences written in 1732, we learn:

Althrop [*sic*] is a fine seat, in the middle of a charming Park, planted with several fine groves (a Rarity in this country) on the skirts of a beautiful down; 'tis moted, but the mote was drained, and turned into a garden so fine, that Monsieur La Quinteney took the plan for some of his works at Versailles.

The apartments in the house are disposed by that excellent genius, the late Earl [Charles]. Besides Family Pictures by Sir Godfrey Kneller, and Sir Peter

Lilly [*sic*], there are some of the best Vandykes, and several Italian Paintings of great value.

Althorp's next chance of promotion from the first division to the premier league of historic houses was not long in coming. Charles's eldest son, Robert, Fourth Earl Sunderland, died abroad when only twenty-eight, a casualty of hard living. This led to another Charles, Fifth Earl of Sunderland, being not only owner of Althorp (which had always been the plan; elder brother Robert was only going to get the Churchill inheritance), but also heir to Blenheim. Perhaps his good fortune went to his head, perhaps he felt he had to leave his mark before moving on to his ducal inheritance; whatever the reason, he ploughed headlong into a four-year spending spree that transformed the Northamptonshire property for ever.

The Wootton Hall has already been examined, and gives a taster of the scale of transformation that the Fifth Earl of Sunderland (as I will call him, so as not to confuse him with his fellow Charles, his father) had in mind. He was determined to show his familiarity with the ancient world, hence the room's Greek allusions, and the frieze incorporating Diana, goddess of hunting. Of course, these expanded on the theme of the equestrian paintings. It is fair to assume that this classical theme would have been continued through the rest of Althorp, should he have remained in charge there for longer.

Outside the house itself, the Fifth Earl of Sunderland had time to build his greatest legacy on the Estate: the Stable Block. John Evelyn had commented in 1675 that, 'There is an old yet honourable gatehouse standing awry, and out-housing mean, but designed to be taken away.' Over half a century later this plan finally came to fruition with the erection of the Stables on the site. At a time when horses were used not only for farmwork, but also for everyday riding, sport and the pulling of carriages, stables were frequently sizeable affairs. Those at Althorp certainly were, as the architect Roger Morris was given complete freedom to execute a truly beautiful Palladian work.

In the opinion of Sarah, Duchess of Marlborough, the Fifth Earl of Sunderland – her grandson – was making a huge and very expensive mistake. She loved Althorp as it was, writing in 1732 that 'there was room enough in it to entertain a King, if one could have so bad a taste

The Stable Block, built in the local yellow ironstone by Charles, Fifth Earl of Sunderland.

as to like them, or the Company that attends them. And yet it was so contriv'd that one might live mighty comfortably with a few friends.' The news that such dramatic alterations were planned for her beloved Althorp was too much for Sarah. In 1733 the old lady vent her spleen in a letter to her favourite granddaughter, Lady Diana Spencer, recently become Duchess of Bedford:

Whatever the expense may be I am sure Allthrop [*sic*] is much the worse for it, and that all which was wanting to make the place the most agreeable habitation that ever I saw was only to make sash windows in the house, and a plain useful stable for thirty or forty horses at most, which is full as many as any man could keep that is not mad, when 'tis become a custom to let strangers' horses go to the inns and this might have been done in a right and useful way for a trifle with the materials of the old stables and the stones I sent

from Holdenby in your brother Robert's time, but I believe there is now built stables for a hundred horses or near it, what can be so ridiculous as this, and to pull down the handsomest and most useful building in the court of Allthrop, and make a very expensive building in the parks which can be of no use . . .

One has to assume that Sarah had not actually seen the Stables, but had merely heard rumours of their cost; she had had run-ins with Morris on her Wimbledon estate over his charges for work there. Moreover, she was furious that Sunderland was spending so much of her beloved Jack Spencer's future inheritance in the process, when he would have Blenheim himself before too long.

Whatever the reasons for Sarah's extreme irritation, it seems improbable that anyone who actually sees the Stables could find fault with the classic Tuscan design, married to the honeyed glow of the ironstone, which was probably quarried from the neighbouring village of Harlestone.

This was a place of work, the clock then on the inside of the courtyard only, its bell chiming every quarter of an hour, to remind the stable staff of how the day was slipping away. In the middle of the courtyard was a fountain, which ensured that the horses' troughs were always filled with water. In one of the rooms overlooking the Deer Park were spaces for hot and cold baths, for the use of riders after a muddy day's hunting. The vet's room still exists, complete with some of the old medicines used for horses; although the gentlemen's smoking room, a nineteenth-century creation, has long gone.

Today the postman comes once in the morning, to deliver, and once in the evening, to collect the mail; still from the Stable Block. In earlier times he had his own stable, where the Harness Room was until early 1998, with horses dedicated solely to his journeys to and from Northampton.

Sarah Marlborough would have been amazed, but the Stable Block proved inadequate for the amount of use that was demanded of it: at the back, out of sight of the main house, two large open sheds were constructed for the everyday carts and carriages. These were not pulled down until 1900.

There was also in this quiet area Lavender Cottage, a wooden

Wendy house where we used to play as children, giving imaginary tea parties for my father and grandmother. Singer, my grandfather's chauffeur, had a son who inadvertently burnt it down, the flames taking to its dry thatched roof with vigour.

Pretty well all the saddles, whips, bridles, even the horses' carved name plates that went outside the individual stable doors, survive to this day. 'Merry Tom', 'Scape Flood' and many other mighty hunters and racers have their own memorials in this way, long after their grooms and stable lads have disappeared into the abyss of anonymity.

Morris clearly borrowed inspiration for the design of his Stables from Inigo Jones's church in Covent Garden, St Paul's; and the only criticism I would have of the building is that it shows up Althorp itself, which has neither the Stables' warmth, nor their beautiful lines. Where the mansion is flat, the Stables benefit from deep and generous porticoes; where the former is cold and reserved, the latter is warm and welcoming. And then there are their respective colours: to have the two edifices so close together is to be able to compare burnished gold with watery silver.

Another beautiful building that was brought to the grounds of Althorp in the four-year tenure of the Fifth Earl of Sunderland was the Gardener's House, now known slightly differently as the Garden House. This is high at the back of the Park, its Palladian design and its ironstone similar to the Stables'. Although the building is really more

The Garden House, home to the head gardener in the eighteenth century.

The Shipwrecked Mariner, now in the main house.

a villa in miniature, it has its own nobility, and it demonstrates the status enjoyed by a head gardener on large country estates in the eighteenth century. The head gardener at Althorp had extensive walled gardens to oversee; they were directly outside his front door, with all manner of fruit, vegetables and flowers cultivated for the big house. Today, you can still see the handsome red-brick walls, and three trees stand to-gether, reminders of what were important ingredients for old-style English cooking: mulberry, medlar and quince.

I know the Garden House well. My early recollection of it stems from my fascination with *The Shipwrecked Mariner*, a melodramatic marble sculpture from the Victorian era. Three-quarter life-sized, it shows a sailor on a broken raft, reaching desperately upwards in a bid

Jack Pettitt, the head gamekeeper, 1972.

to be plucked from the sea after the sinking of his ship. This used to lie in the main portico of the Garden House, but the recent fad for stealing statues and garden ornaments persuaded me to bring him down into the main house, where his outstretched palm and terror-stricken eyes can be appreciated for the unadulterated Victoriana that they are.

I used to slip up to the Garden House as a boy to see Jack, the head gamekeeper, who lived there with his wife, children and spaniels. Jack was a great charmer, his blue eyes always mirroring his smile. They say he pretty much helped himself to the fruits of the game larder, selling venison for his own benefit when perhaps he should not have, but he always stayed on the right side of my grandfather, and my father and I liked him enormously.

The Fifth Earl of Sunderland can have had no idea of the diversity of occupant that his 'Gardener's House' would have, two and a half centuries on. My sister Jane and her family used it for ten years during my father's time; my niece Laura's apple tree finally producing fruit now. And then there was a more exotic stage, after my former step-mother had transformed it from rural simplicity into an explosion of chintz, frilly blinds and extremely strong wallpapers. One tenant was a lady whose brother expressed an interest in playing for my cricket team – he played a bit, he said, for his own team, 'the Lazarusians' ('We have all,' he confided, 'to a greater or lesser degree, risen from the dead'). His name was Peter O'Toole. This gave me an uncommon advantage on the cricket pitch over any other captain because, if ever an opposing batting partnership was proving a bit too threatening, I could simply summon up Lawrence of Arabia with his artillery – in Peter's case, gentle swing bowling which, although not as dramatic as an all-out attack on Aqaba, was highly effective in its own theatrical way.

Later Diana had her heart set on the Garden House as a rural retreat from Kensington Palace, after her separation. Sadly, consideration of security and the protection of my young children from press intrusion made me rule this out after much thought. Although I offered her any number of other properties on the Estate – including Wormleighton Manor, which would have been more suitable on every front – this rare refusal in her adult life led to a brief but bitter silence from her. I suppose it is a tribute to Morris's art and Sunderland's taste that, for Diana, there was just no alternative to their Palladian jewel.

On 18 October 1994, I gathered a variety of Spencer relatives at Althorp for a simple service in the Chapel. We were there to mark the 250th anniversary of the death, at the age of eighty-eight, of Sarah Marlborough. One of the great female characters of British history, Sarah was also benefactor supreme of my family. Afterwards there was a luncheon party in the house, with the Marlborough Silver on display – the most obviously dazzling legacy she left her Spencer heirs. We then heard a brief talk from Frances Harris, Sarah's biographer, about what it was that drove this extraordinary woman, who was part-courtier, part-businesswoman, part-politician and one hundred per cent independent.

Sarah was not an easy woman, except in her unreserved love for her husband. By the latter years of her life, she was chained to a cycle of severe fallings-out with her plethora of titled grandchildren. At one family gathering she likened herself to the roots of a tree, with her family as the branches springing from her; to which one of her grandchildren rejoindered that this was undoubtedly so since, like all branches, they would only flourish once the roots were buried. It is said that she changed her will fifty times, depending on who was out of favour at the time. Certainly, it was a will worth being included in.

By the time of her death she had amassed thirty landed estates in twelve counties, all but two of them in the years of her widowhood. Her art collection was similarly magnificent, the cream of it residing in her mansions at Wimbledon and Holywell in St Albans. The works by Hondecoeter, Snyders and Kneller were famously fine, and highly fashionable at the start of the eighteenth century. Sir Godfrey Kneller, court painter to Queen Anne, captured a variety of likenesses of Sarah. It was to him that she came after a fierce quarrel with her husband, to be painted, her eyes swollen with tearful rage, her beautiful long auburn hair cut off, held half-defiantly, half-pathetically, in her hands.

Sarah Jennings, First Duchess of Marlborough, by Sir Godfrey Kneller.

Sarah had also made a point of collecting the very finest jewellery, including a celebrated diamond necklace, one of the most famous creations of its day. Less spectacular, and acquired by Sarah for £500, was a pair of pearls that had captured the imagination of early eighteenth-century English society because of their provenance: they had originally been given to Elizabeth of Bohemia by the City of London and were passed on to her son, Prince Rupert of the Rhine, who bequeathed them to his mistress. They are still at Althorp today.

The Marlborough Silver in the 1880s in Dublin, where John Poyntz,
Fifth Earl Spencer, was serving as Viceroy of Ireland.

There was also the Marlborough Silver, an accumulation of the pilgrim bottles, plates, dishes, cisterns, candlesticks and wine cisterns that the First Duke of Marlborough took on his European campaigns during the War of the Spanish Succession. To see them is to marvel at the stately pace at which military wagon trains must have travelled then, and to realize the extraordinary level of comfort commanders-in-chief of the time enjoyed.

The early part of the collection was given to the Duke to enhance his status by the States General of Holland since he acted as their Ambassador Extraordinary. Most spectacular is the 46-inch wine cistern, which weighs close to 2,000 ounces, made by the Huguenot goldsmith, Philip Rollos. It cost over £1,000 300 years ago. This would have held ice or snow from an ice-house, in which wine was chilled. Once the wine and dinner were finished, it would double up as a sink, where the plates would be washed. It's strange to think of such a majestic and highly valuable piece of silver being used for such a mundane task once the party was over.

Another Huguenot, Pierre Harache, crafted a slightly lesser wine cistern, as well as a stunning pair of rosewater ewers and dishes. John Goode was responsible for a pair of pilgrim bottles, whereas the other pair came to Colonel Churchill, as Marlborough was in the mid-1670s, ironically, possibly as gifts from his eventual arch-enemy, Louis XIV, after Churchill had led the English Regiment to victory in the storming of Maastricht. These complete the display of major items, when the collection is on show. Later pieces were rewards for his most celebrated victories; after Blenheim, his greatest triumph, Queen Anne added significantly to the value and variety of the ensemble, particularly with a pair of gold ice-pails that were reputed to be the greatest in private hands in England.

All the above was left to Jack Spencer, despite its being very much 'the Marlborough Silver', which would suggest that it should by rights have gone to Blenheim. With this influx of riches, so soon after the Second Earl of Sunderland's great additions, Althorp became one of the great treasure houses of Europe.

We have seen the short enjoyment Jack Spencer had of his wealth, dying within two years of his doting grandmother. Perhaps there was some justice in this, because he never really liked her, and had on many occasions shirked from an honest showdown with the manipulative old meddler to secure a decent share of her wealth. We have also tasted the extravagance and generosity of his son, John, First Earl Spencer, through the celebrations of his coming of age. And yet, despite the staggering wealth of the Spencer family at this time, Althorp was suffering: there were too many distractions, and nobody was taking care of the basics, the fabric. Guests complained that their bedroom ceilings were leaking. The brickwork was clearly decaying fast. By 1783, when the First Earl was succeeded by George John, Second Earl Spencer, Althorp was in an advanced state of deterioration. Indeed, its very survival was in question.

The *Northampton Mercury* of 22 June 1772 carried an urgent announcement:

LABOURERS: Wanted immediately at Althorp near Northampton a number of good labourers that have been used to serve masons and bricklayers; the Wages are ten shillings a week and to work from five in the morning till seven in the evening. None need apply but those that have been used to climbing and are willing to work.

N.B. Ten or a Dozen Bricklayers and Masons are likewise wanted and good wages will be allowed them.

Whatever work happened in the wake of this call for help, it was not enough. The First Earl Spencer, remembered for all time as the creator of one of London's finest private palaces, Spencer House, was, ironically, guilty of neglecting the property that should have been his prime material consideration, Althorp. Even his own mother was furious that rain water could not be kept out of her dressing room, the very room where her son and daughter-in-law were secretly wed. Next door to that, the ceiling of the original Library actually collapsed in 1773. Around the same time a new floor was put down in the Picture Gallery, since the existing one, too, was found to be unsafe. Althorp was falling apart.

We live in an age when we hear endless tales of great houses falling into disrepair because the families that have historically owned them can sadly no longer afford the great expense of maintenance. Pretty much without exception, this state of affairs is reached after every effort has been made to keep things going for as long as possible. It is therefore extraordinary for us to learn that one of the richest dynasties in the country did not bother to look after its principal residence.

George John resolved to put matters right. He needed to find an architect to oversee the repairs. Henry Holland was a name George

Henry Holland, responsible for the transformation of Althorp which began in 1788.

John would have known well. In 1771 Holland had been instrumental in the construction of Battersea Bridge for the First Earl Spencer. Seventeen years later the construction of Brooks's Club in St James's Street, London, confirmed to George John that Holland's was a talent that could be well employed. At first Holland was entrusted in 1785 with some 'renewing and repairing' work at Spencer House; and then he was asked to design something suitable to help salvage Althorp.

There is no doubt that George John was feeling more than a little bit tentative about the project at Althorp, when he first met Holland on site

Lady Lavinia Bingham, by Sir Joshua Reynolds 1782.

in 1786. He had been master of the house for only three years, and he was still facing the prospect of having to deal with his father's electioneering and Spencer House debts. George John's wife, Lavinia, was similarly concerned at the cost of the proposed work: 'I must say Holland frightens me – but 'tis easy to lay him and his estimate in a drawer and take them out when we are Croesus's,' she said. Four months later, on

George John, Second Earl Spencer, with his sisters, by Angelica Kauffman.

Althorp, by John Vosterman, 1677. This shows the original red brick before it was tiled. To the right is Holdenby House, where Charles I was imprisoned and arrested.

22 December 1786, George John's own financial insecurities were laid bare in a letter to his mother, Georgiana (she of the secret wedding):

We have also got Mr Holland here, who has brought the plans with him, which I am to see this morning. I have a notion they would be very clever ones to put in execution but the Quomodo is the difficulty, and in my present circumstances I must be contented with making the apartment we live in weatherproof, which it really hardly is at present, and saving the rest of the house from tumbling down, which in part was very near happening t'other day in the high wind when part of the balustrade round the top came down just before the door of the little Dining Room and if anybody had been there, would infallibly have killed them . . .

So, from these modest beginnings – more a desire for preservation than for reconstruction – stemmed the overhaul that was to transform

64

Althorp into a Georgian mansion, in which every room, except the Wootton Hall, was changed by the highly fashionable Mr Holland.

There is every sign that Holland was extremely keen on this particular commission and, sensing George John's reservations about costs (the 'Quomodo' so coyly referred to above), offered to fund some of the work himself, provided he was repaid in full with commission. This was a trick he had learned from his father-in-law, 'Capability' Brown, who had also had problems collecting the money owed by even the grandest clients. Unfortunately, this was not the only idea passed on by the unquestioned king of landscaping.

Before Brown, red brick was a common material for the construction of important country houses. Certainly, to the modern eye, the old red-brick exterior of Althorp is classically beautiful, as shown in the handsome painting by John Vosterman in the present Billiard Room, dating from the mid seventeenth century. However, Brown, with his enormous influence, was of the opinion that 'a red house puts the whole valley in a fever'. This belief spelt doom for the red exterior of Althorp.

Holland's choice for the task of transforming the exterior of the house was a white brick, but this proposal was deemed too expensive. A 'mathematical' tile was then considered; a flat creation which could simply encase the red brick without any great structural changes. This proved acceptable to patron and client, and the tiles were made in a kiln near Ipswich.

A slightly grander touch was given to the exterior by the four Corinthian pilasters at the front of Althorp, made from hardy Roche Abbey stone, which was brought from Yorkshire. Apparently Sir Christopher Wren had originally wanted to build St Paul's Cathedral from this same material. And so it was that the cladding of Althorp started in earnest in 1788.

At the time the result was greeted with almost universal approval. One visitor, in 1789, was a Miss Rachel Lloyd, who wrote to the Dowager Countess Spencer: 'I twice went to Althrope [sic], it is quite astonishing what they have already done and I really think when it is quite finished, it will be one of the most complete fine comfortable places in England.' But Horace Walpole's was a lone voice of dissension: 'I am sorry that pretty outside is demolished and that

65

Mr Holland has so much of the spirit of a lucrative profession in him as to prefer destroying to not being employed.'

I have to agree with Walpole. To be fair, the mathematical tiles probably were a wise solution to the problem of advanced decay; but they certainly have contributed to the house's stark appearance ever since. I always used to dream of peeling back the tiles to liberate the Tudor house; but I have seen what lies underneath, and the weathering is too advanced to make it possible for such a dream to become reality. Furthermore, the nails used to fasten the tiles on to the brick have compounded the damage dramatically.

And that is without considering the really practical problems posed by Holland's additions, most notably the parallel corridors in the front courtyard, running along the outside of the old house: before these were added, people would have had to walk from room to room, passing through each one on the way to their final destination. As privacy became more of a priority, and as rooms started to be cast less flexibly in their roles – before the eighteenth century nearly any room in the main part of the house was used at one time or other for dining in, for example – corridors became more desirable. Before Holland, there was no 'Painter's Passage', parallel to what are currently the Library, Billiard Room or South Drawing Room: what is now passage was then courtyard. Similarly, what is today the Green Passage, on the opposite side of the courtyard, was also external. We know from old engravings that the two great wings of the house had immeasurably more elegance, when viewed from the front, before Holland.

There were many other alterations which modern tastes may judge to be desecrations rather than improvements. The Picture Gallery suffered the indignity of having its fine oak panelling covered in white paint, which was in turn entombed in a layer of canvas, with wallpaper over that. Later generations of the family assumed that Holland had actually removed the oak. It took Edward Anderson, house carpenter at the start of this century, to notice oak above the chimney piece while effecting some minor repairs. In 1904 the panelling, canvas and white paint were prised off to return the Picture Gallery to how it should always have been; this restoration was funded by the sale of a painting in the housekeeper's room which, fortunately, turned out to be a lost Rubens. (The £2,000 this lucky find brought in paid not only for

The Green Passage.

the reconstitution of a mighty room, but also for its very first central heating system.)

But, if we need proof that Holland was only obeying the fashion dictats of the day, and was not simply imposing his own regrettable tastes on gullible clients, we find it in a letter of 1792 from George, Fourth Earl of Jersey, to the Dowager Countess Spencer:

Last week I went to Althorp from Wakefield Lodge and though you had said how much had been done to the house, and how comfortable it had been made, I did not really conceive it possible that such a change could have been effected, either in the cheerfulness of the outside or the convenient disposition of the rooms within. I did recollect the spaces and that was all I could do. The planners have shown much skill and the furnishing is quite full of taste.

This enthusiasm was shared by George John and his wife, Lavinia, who trilled that 'The Gallery is now a beautiful lightsome room.' This despite the fact that Holland had actually blocked in the windows at the end of the Picture Gallery, which overlooked the front of the house. But the other windows were widened by Holland, as they were throughout the house; something which would have pleased Marchioness Grey, a visitor in 1748, who had carped: 'The rooms ... are rather dark, and the reverse of *cheerful* though not amounting to *dismal* which is occasioned by its not being sashed.'

Other ways of brightening up the house that Holland considered clever, but which may appear cavalier to us, were painting the main, walnut staircase in the Saloon – one of the principal features of the interior of the house – white. Fortunately this effect was removed half a century later.

Holland also set to work outside, driving his bill up to a phenomenal £20,000 in total, by eradicating any trace of the old moat and draining the lake in the Deer Park, which the First Earl had used as a playground for his full-sized Venetian gondolas. At the same time the grass lawns were brought right up to the walls of the mansion.

But if there was a triumph among all the minor disasters of Holland's influence, it lay in what his patron would have viewed as the core of the house: the Library. For generations this room had seemed out of proportion, appearing too long for its height. Holland added alcoves on both ends, which tapered in either side of the room, while simultaneously creating extra room for the ever-growing book collection. This was the beginning of the century in which the Library would be the dominant room at Althorp.

The Library.

The Library tells the story of the Spencer's fortunes in the eighteenth and nineteenth centuries most eloquently. The family had long been interested in books. We have already seen that the Earls of Sunderland had a magnificent library in their London house, and a lesser – but still excellent – one at Althorp. Before that their sheep-farming ancestors had emphasized their appreciation of culture by collecting early English literature at Wormleighton.

John, First Earl Spencer, added to the family collection; most spectacularly when he bought the entire library of Dr William George, a headmaster of Eton. Again, these works were primarily English.

It was George John, Holland's patron, who transformed the Spencer Library into the greatest private collection of books in England; probably in Europe. Judging by the full-length Reynolds portrait of him as an eighteen-year-old student at Trinity College, Cambridge, in which he holds a book by his side, George John's interest in literature started at an early age. By the end of his life, it had become an obsession.

The cornerstone of the collection – and one which added Greek and Latin classics to his English inheritance – was his acquisition in 1790 of Count Reviczky's collection. When we come to see the figures spent on later purchases, George John got a bargain here, with a down payment of £1,000, and an annual payment for the duration of the Count's life of £500. Fortunately for the Earl, and unfortunately for the Count, Reviczky died after only three years of this arrangement.

By the time of his own death in 1834, George John was an expert on all manner of books in his own right. From 1802, though, he enjoyed the enthusiastic guidance of the Reverend Thomas Frognall Dibdin, whose *Aedes Althorpianae* catalogues the contents of the house, concentrating on the ever-burgeoning shelves of the Library:

The Library at Althorp occupies a suite of apartments, on the ground floor;

George John, Second Earl Spencer, by Sir Joshua Reynolds, 1786.

of which the entire length – from the extremity of the first apartment, called 'The Long Library', to that of the fifth or last apartment, called 'The Gothic Library' – cannot be less than two hundred and twenty feet. These rooms may be said, with very few exceptions, to be filled with books to the very ceiling.

When he wrote this, Dibdin was official librarian at Althorp. It was largely thanks to his influence and encouragement that George John's original collection, which was housed comfortably in the Long Library in the mid-1790s, had extended to the five libraries mentioned above. Even these were soon to be insufficient; within a few years of Dibdin's writing the above, the entire 115-foot Picture Gallery had its lower walls lined with full bookshelves.

George John was an active politician, serving Pitt as First Lord of the Admiralty, during which time he befriended Nelson, and promoted him over the heads of his senior colleagues, to the subsequent regret of Napoleon's navy. While in the Cabinet, he bought books as a hobby. When he retired from public life in 1807, he devoted his energy and talent to his favourite pursuit, in particular, collecting the works of William Caxton, of which he managed to acquire fifty-seven, four of which were unique. By the time of his death, he owned 110,000 volumes.

George John was keen to give his library the widest possible subject base: it is said that in the final decade of his life he ordered a copy of every book published in England. This was not simply to be a classical collection; even though the first vastly expensive work we hear of him buying, for £750, was a copy of the Valdarfer Boccaccio. Another great rarity that came to Althorp was a woodcut of St Christopher, dated 1423, at the time believed to be the oldest example of a work in ink that includes the date of its creation on it. This was one of nine 'block books' in the Spencer Library.

Add to this Papal Letters of Indulgence from 1452, the first edition of the 'Mazarin' Bible of 1455 and the Mentz Psalter of 1457, and you begin to realize that this was an extraordinarily rare collection. The very earliest works from the printing presses at Augsburg and Nuremberg, *Bonaventurae Meditationes* and *Comestorium Vitiorum* respectively, also found their way to Northamptonshire.

George John was not the only aristocrat interested in improving his library. This was brought home to him at the sale of the Duke of Roxburgh's books in 1812, when George John and his cousin, the Duke of Marlborough, got caught up in a bidding war for Boccaccio's *Decameron*, of 1471, of which only three copies were known to exist. Neither man wanted to give way; but George John pulled out when Marlborough bid the ludicrous figure of £2,260. It must have given him enormous satisfaction to get the same book, when Marlborough later sold it on, for £750!

But George John was haemorrhaging money on books by this stage, at a time when his income was being squeezed by the great agricultural depression triggered by the Napoleonic Wars. There was also the strain of his great expenditure on entertaining, for Althorp became a centre of culture during this time: the actor David Garrick was an especially close friend, spending one Christmas with George John and Lavinia at Althorp, and then there were Johnson, Gibbon, Sheridan and Reynolds. All formed part of the 'salon' that the Spencers delighted in, and would not have thought of looking after except in the most sumptuous manner.

By a lucky stroke George John was to be succeeded by one of the few heirs to the great estates of the time who was not interested in perpetuating great extravagance; one who also had a remarkably firm grasp of fiscal discipline – John Charles, Viscount Althorp, the Leader of the House of Commons during the passing of the Reform Bill of 1832, and Chancellor of the Exchequer. He had an exceptional relationship with his father and, even when he must have realized that his inheritance was being reduced, just as the book collection increased, he made it clear that he was not resentful of the Library's place in his father's affections.

I have often wondered whether this solid, decent man ever regretted his letter of 1813, where he wrote to his father: 'I am not much afraid at my future prospects being at your mercy. Do as you please.' George John certainly needed no encouragement, and it is no surprise to find that, at the time of his death, having rebuilt Althorp, bought an estate on the Isle of Wight, another in Northamptonshire at Harlestone, bought paintings, and amassed the premier Library in the kingdom, while living like a medieval prince, he passed John Charles the small matter of a £500,000 debt. This, when the entire income of the Estate was £40,000; and that mortgaged to the extent that the new Third Earl Spencer had a spendable income of £7,500. A hundred years earlier, remember, his great-grandfather had four times that, with no debts and endless capital reserves.

Now it would have appeared reasonable for John Charles to have 'cashed in' the Library at this point. It was, after all, the chief culprit for his sorry position, and its sale would have covered his debts. But to the dutiful son it would have been sacrilege to have contemplated such a disrespectful move against his father's great love: the Library was to remain intact, and economies would have to be made elsewhere. John Charles told his financial adviser, John Shaw Lefevre: 'Decision and firmness are required. The first I have. I am a little doubtful whether I have the second.'

John Charles, Third Earl Spencer, by George Hayter.

It was unfortunate, to say the least, that this decisiveness resulted in the sale of three London boroughs. But go they did – Battersea, Putney and Wimbledon, before they were more than mere south London hamlets. And yet I admire the plodding honesty of John Charles as he tackled the unpleasant task of dealing with the debt, which process he called 'the great operation'. He had not only Althorp to maintain, but also his mansions at Wimbledon and Spencer House, his farm at Wiseton, and his shooting retreat in Norfolk. Althorp alone, with its forty servants in the house and fifty in the Park, cost £5,000 per year to maintain. He therefore moved out, the first Spencer to do so, and lived for most of the year at Wiseton, his late wife's ancestral home, whose annual maintenance was a more palatable £1,200. Here John Charles, who was one of the founders of the Royal Agricultural Society, oversaw his one extravagance – a herd of prize bulls.

So Althorp remained deserted, even the fallow deer herd being dispersed, sent away from their ancestral home. It took four months to round them up, the bucks having their horns sawn off, to make them easier to transport away in vans. Most went to King William IV, who sent them to Windsor, Richmond and Bushey; others went to local landowners at Hagley, Kelmarsh, Boughton and Cottesbrooke.

John Charles went still further, with even the gardens being leased out. Only one servant was designated to occupy and tend the house; reinforced only during the few weeks per year when John Charles camped in one wing, in order to fulfil his duty – his whole life, poor man, was one of seemingly unremitting duty – sitting in the Quarter Sessions in Northampton.

The one thing he was sure of was that the Library must not be sold. He tried to find a buyer for Spencer House, even, but nobody wanted to take on such an expensive proposition. He sold farm land in Buckinghamshire and Bedfordshire. He parted with the mansion at Wimbledon, as well as the Isle of Wight property. But the books had to stay, out of loyalty to his father.

Thanks to his belief that the best investment was the paying off of debts, and thanks to his unfailing thrift, by the time of his own death, a childless widower, in 1845, he left an Estate that was in credit, without any debt whatsoever. More than that, he left an asset, in the Library, that was to be Althorp's saviour soon enough.

Frederick, Fourth Earl Spencer, had never expected to inherit Althorp. He was the fourth son of George John, and became a naval officer, not an unexpected career choice for an aristocratic younger son, especially since his father had been a highly successful First Lord of the Admiralty. However, the death without children of his three elder brothers meant that the admiral, as he then was, who had

Frederick, Fourth Earl Spencer, by S. Catterson Smith.

also been a Member of Parliament, found himself the owner of a large, buoyant inheritance.

He never forgot the limited funds at his disposal during his years as an unimportant younger son. A strict, humourless man, in a letter of 1856 he reminded his eldest son of what it had been like to be a victim of primogeniture's harsh discriminations:

I do not wish to boast, but what can be more useful to a Son than to know the longer experience of his Father and I am certain you will understand the object wherefore I tell you that I began life a younger son with £150 a year when I was a Lieutenant which was doubled when I became 21. I went on with that allowance until I commanded the 'Talbot', I once got into debt and my father cleared me, it was as well to remember under £200, but the misery I underwent was so great I determined to avoid such a position in future and I accomplished the point so that for years even up to your birth I had to contend with considerable difficulties and to restrain many desires but I had no misery as to debt for I never was in it . . . I thank God that I am spared long enough to be able to advise you and be assured you will not reject the advice which I give in truth and sincerity for your good – It is as to expenses short and in one sentence, viz. 'Keep out of debt'.

Frederick, Fourth Earl Spencer, with the head coachman.

Frederick died the following year, his twelve-year tenure of Althorp being devoid of any dramatic changes; as you would expect from a man with such a thrifty creed. He did have a taste for fine china, and for Japanese furniture, neither of which had interested his forebears as much as books and paintings, and his collection can still be seen at Althorp. It was also Frederick who removed Holland's white paint from the Saloon, staining the walnut staircase to match the surrounding oak. But, in the main, he followed the example set by his eldest brother, John Charles, and kept everything, including the Library, together. One reversal he did implement was securing a deer herd for Althorp again, buying beasts from Dingley Park. Their descendants are still at Althorp, with Frederick's.

The only actual extravagance I have associated with my great-great-grandfather relates to his Knight of the Garter jewellery. Like his father and his son, Frederick was made a member of this exclusive order of chivalry; quite unexpectedly, according to contemporary accounts. Soon after I inherited, I was going through some supposedly empty leather boxes in Althorp. There was one locked box, in battered purple leather, which had no key. I noticed what looked like flakes of bright red nail varnish near the keyhole, where someone had presumably tried to prise it open; but opening the case was a job for Ken Wilkin, Estate carpenter and all-round improviser, who neatly sawed through the lock.

Inside, encased in sumptuous velvet, lay the various symbols of the Garter jewellery, as worn by Frederick: diamonds picked out the motto of the order, '*Honi soit qui mal y pense*', on the actual garter, and yet more diamonds joined rubies and sapphires on the brooch, and lesser items. It is a relief to know that behind the austere exterior of the man there was a weakness: vanity.

John, Fifth Earl Spencer, was known as 'the Red Earl' on account of the colour of his magnificent beard. It was to him that the lifeline of the Library was to be thrown, as he encountered the same problems as George John: natural extravagance and a declining agricultural income. The latter impacted hard on him, since his 27,000 acres, all but

John Poyntz, Fifth Earl Spencer, 'the Red Earl', by Frank Holl.

10,000 of them in Northamptonshire, were his only source of revenue. It says a lot about the depression in farming at the end of the nineteenth century that even such a vast tract of farmland was inadequate for the Red Earl's needs. It also says a fair amount about his not having taken his father's strictures on debt to heart.

The Red Earl was married to Charlotte Seymour, a great beauty fondly called 'Spencer's Fairy Queen'. Together they made a glittering couple, and at a young age they were sent by Gladstone to be the Viceroy and Vicereine of Ireland, resulting in only fleeting visits back to Althorp, from 1868 to 1874. Although there was an income that went with the post, it never matched the expenditure that was demanded by

John Poyntz, Fifth Earl Spencer, with his wife Charlotte, Countess Spencer, relaxing during a rifle shoot on Wimbledon Common, by Sir Henry Tamworth Wells.

it: endless entertainment was inevitable, not that the Spencers minded. They threw themselves into the business of making their official home, Dublin Castle, the venue for frequent balls, dinners and banquets.

In March 1871 the Red Earl reported to Lord Hartington, Irish Secretary, exactly how expensive life as Viceroy was proving to be. He started his letter in apologetic tones: 'The Castle expenditure is always huge from the large Balls and dinners which must be given. I feel ashamed at the figure.' The cost of moving his thirty-one servants with him to Dublin and back, with six carriages and thirty horses, was, when added to the transporting of silver, linen and furniture, a bearable £400. However, Spencer then estimated the 'Cost of living a month at

Charlotte Spencer in 1885.

the Viceregal Lodge, calculated from a month in which there was a Zingari Ball, some cricket matches and other entertainments', at nearly £1,500.

The Red Earl explained what, precisely, had contributed to the expenses of that, typical, month: an average of 226 meals per day, with the understanding that 'a luncheon or a ball-supper [is] calculated as half a meal'; and the maintenance of the stables, at over £100 per month – 'The calculation of stable expenditure includes the keep of 36 horses, the expenses necessary to hunting, the pay of grooms, coachmen, and helpers, and their board wages . . .'

These years in Ireland were successful politically, as was shown by the Red Earl being reappointed to the position in 1882, as well as being offered a promotion from earl to marquess on his retirement from the post; but they were not good news for Althorp. The only way it benefited tangibly was in the acquisition of the three most beautiful chandeliers in the house, made in Dublin, and now in the Sunderland Room and my bedroom. Lovely though they are, they are not much of a return on the tens of thousands of Victorian pounds the Red Earl spent in order to create the right impression as bountiful Viceroy.

In 1874 Gladstone's government fell, and the Red Earl returned to Althorp. Within two years the Spencers had decided to embark on what was to become Althorp's last major reorganization. Exactly as George John, the Red Earl shirked from the expense of the project, telling his wife in a letter of August 1876:

I have had the estimates for the Althorp alterations and they are anything but agreeable. The lowest is close upon £19,000 and this does not cover painting, decorating, gables, chimney-pieces, bell-hanging, etc.

I will not settle until I see you but I confess that I think the sensible thing will be to give up the large changes.

My feeling is this. We never have spare cash and the last two or three years have been rather living beyond our income. An addition of income of £1,000 would be a great help.

Moreover, the House is really very comfortable. Our predecessors for two generations have gone on without change, and it is not a change of absolute necessity.

...We shall not get off under £25,000 even £30,000 and this is a small

The Great Dining Room, created by J. MacVicar Anderson, was added by the Fifth Earl in 1877.

fortune. This is a dear time. Perhaps in five or six years building may be cheaper.

I am satisfied that this is the prudent and most sensible view.

It may well have been so, but it was not a view that the Red Earl could adhere to. That year, 1876, the alterations to Althorp commenced in earnest. The most successful was pushing the end of the Saloon back twenty feet: prior to this there had been a servant's room between what is now the fireplace and several yards into the Saloon. This intervening wall was pulled down, and the Saloon acquired a grandeur that had previously been rather compressed.

Also, the Great Dining Room was added to the side of the house. A double cube, this magnificent room was supposedly a copy of the ballroom in Buckingham Palace, and was created by MacVicar Anderson. It is not a room I have ever warmed to; although it was beautiful in Grandfather's day, its walls hung with faded, red damask silk. Despite the redness, it was never a warm room, feeling like the late addition to Althorp that it is, rather than a part of its main body.

I suppose I also have a personal antipathy to the place, as it was the room in which I got my first hangover, when I was just eight years old.

My grandfather had a party in there to celebrate his eightieth birthday, and one of the guests made me drink a glass of champagne. Great-aunt Delia took me into the Tapestry Dining Room to cool off. According to Mr Pendrey the butler, I said to her, 'You look like a pig.' She turned to him and with a beatific smile said, 'Isn't he sweet?!' Poor, dear, octogenarian Aunt Delia; her hearing was never her strong point.

The drive back to my father's house in Norfolk late that night, I do not remember. The severe telling-off from my nanny the next day, as I lay in bed feeling bilious, I can sadly recall in detail. My father looked on, trying not to let slip that he found the whole thing very amusing.

But for the Red Earl this room was a serious improvement. Prior to its being built, the main dining room had been in what is now the South Drawing Room; absurdly, the furthest room on the ground floor from the kitchens. Meanwhile, a breakfast room was being built to the right of the Wootton Hall; what is now the Tapestry Dining Room. The emphasis of the Red Earl's work was on making the mansion both comfortable and practical.

During the 1876–8 improvements the Red Earl and his wife moved into Harlestone House, a mile from Althorp. It no longer exists, although its park still does, now one of three golf courses in the area. The Spencers enjoyed moving back to what had been the Red Earl's childhood home during the time of his uncle, John Charles, at Althorp. When the Red Earl and Charlotte first thought of moving back at the end of 1878, it proved two things: first, that the changes were every bit as extensive as the Red Earl had initially promised himself they would not be; and, secondly, that the couple had been right to move out. In October the Red Earl reported to Charlotte:

The confusion, noise and smells here are beyond conception.

Our wing will be quite finished in a fortnight.

The panelling in your bedroom looks very well. It is finished but wants paint. How is it to be painted?

The servants' Hall and your sitting room will all be ready about the same time. They are painting the ceiling in the Long Library, also the Tea room and Chapel stairs.

The floor of the West ground floor corridor behind the old Drawing and Dining Room is quite rotten and must all be taken up.

The staircase is getting on. The chimney piece is being put up. The floor is not down nor is that of the Dining room, but in a few days we can use that part of the stairs going across from the Entrance Hall to the breakfast room, so we shall be able to use the top of the stairs.

All the attics, the blue rooms and my room are prepared and finished and look very well.

I live in the Domenichino and Breakfast Room, have to walk along the Long Library to get up to the Gallery.

You would go mad so don't come except for Sunday.

And then, a brittle reminder of what was expected of her as chatelaine, in the stark post scriptum: 'You are wanted to decide paint.' At least Charlotte can have been in no doubt as to where her responsibilities began and ended.

Either side of the modifications at Althorp, the couple continued to entertain on a scale that can only be termed lavish. Elizabeth, Empress of Austria, was a regular house guest, and the Spencers never stinted when she came to stay. Similarly, the Red Earl was an exceptionally keen fox-hunter, being Master of the Pytchley Hounds, on which he spent enormous sums. He was determined that the Pytchley should become the most respected of hunts, and a particular pleasure for him was having his favourite hound, 'Forager', being voted the best foxhound in England. There cannot be many other late-eighteenth-century dogs whose master had their likeness cast, life-sized, in bronze. He stands today in the Billiard Room at Althorp, tail erect, waiting in vain for someone to score a century break.

'Forager', the Fifth Earl's favourite foxhound, cast in bronze.

By the 1890s the North American prairies had opened up, and English agriculture was no longer the provider of income that it had been. The Red Earl, hunting and entertaining debts mounting, his inability to economize constant, decided that a dramatic capital sale was required; and the Library, built up by the Second Earl, left intact by the Third and Fourth, was earmarked for disposal.

I look at this, a century on, and of course I feel sad. But I have come to understand that this neat amputation was the right solution at the time. I am only grateful that it was an option; that John Charles had not contemplated selling it, and that it was therefore an avenue open to the Red Earl who, having failed to heed his father's admonishments about over-expenditure, needed to find ready cash in order to be able to hold on to Althorp at all.

Beyond that, generations of visitors had complained that it was bordering on the iniquitous that a library so fine had been confined to the distant county of Northamptonshire. It was therefore a consolation to all involved when a wealthy widow, Mrs Rylands, came forward offering to buy the Library as a whole, for a collection in Manchester to commemorate her husband. The books were therefore to remain together and to become much more accessible; crumbs of comfort to the Red Earl, as he explained to Charlotte in a letter of July 1892:

I was very sad over the books I confess ... I must have the rooms photographed. It is a great thing that they should be kept together and for the Public and this would not have been done unless the lot had gone together. I should have got a great deal less and they would have been scattered to the four quarters of the world ... But I feel it is a great pity.

It was decided that a few books, of particular importance to the family, would be held on to. Among these were a series of volumes of Shakespeare's works, illustrated by the Second Earl's mother-in-law, Lady Lucan. Also, Sarah, Duchess of Marlborough's family Bible, which lists every member of the Spencer family after her, naming their date of birth, date and place of christening, godparents, date and place of marriage, spouse, children and date of death. I recently had to bring it up to date.

The rest went; all five rooms of it. It must have been devastating to the Red Earl, with his highly developed sense of responsibility, to see the eyes being plucked out of the Althorp collection. Charlotte tried to make it all all right, going off on excursions to Daventry and Chesham, North Creake and Norwich to try to fill the empty shelves. It soon

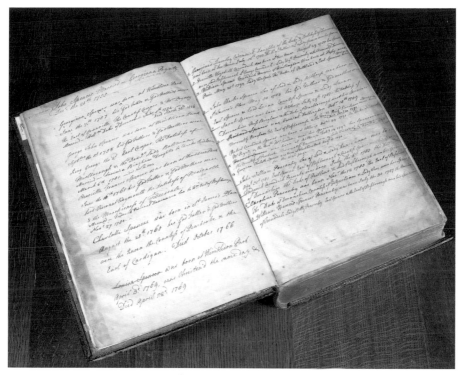

A page from the family bible. The first entry, still legible:
'John Spencer, married Georgiana Poyntz, 20th December 1755'.

became clear that it was going to be impossible to replace the gaps in all the different libraries, so they decided to concentrate on the Long Library, Holland's great success in the house, which was used in the evenings as the main drawing room, and which was, after all, as big as most private libraries in the country.

Although this was successfully done, I do not believe the Red Earl ever forgave himself for selling the Library. From 1892 his correspondence betrays an obsession with acquiring books; and the sadness is, these never approached the quality of those that had gone; not surprising, really, since the Red Earl allowed himself only 'an average' to be spent on each acquisition. There is something pathetic about the one-time owner of the greatest private library in Europe writing to his wife:

I had a great success yesterday in buying books and got 42 volumes but unluckily was tempted with two dear ones, so my average was up. One of the expensive books was worth buying, three volumes of Daniel's Field Sports with coloured illustrations of birds, dogs, fish, etc. £3.15./. The cheapest book I bought was one excellent edition of Bacon's works, small folios, four volumes at 15./ . . .

So the Library was finally gone, less than a century after it had been started in earnest, a symbol of the varying fortunes of the English upper classes in the nineteenth century, and, more specifically, of Althorp and its occupants.

It would be wrong to see all the Red Earl's expenditure as mere extravagance: the house was certainly improved during his time; in 1899 it was even adapted to take electric light. But the outside, the Park and gardens, also changed dramatically in the second half of the nineteenth century. It was to be one of the last chapters in the history of the area surrounding the mansion.

As you enter the West Lodge, on the Brington road, you will see that the grazing land on the right is pitted and bumpy, in contrast to the smoothness of the rest of the Park. This is where the old village of Oldthorpe was. It probably ceased to exist as a result of the Black Death, in the mid fourteenth century, when the population of England was decimated by rat-carried plague.

Human activity from an even earlier period is visible throughout the Park in the ridge and furrow roll of the land. Saxon farmers used this method, creating high, parallel troughs and crests in the land, maximizing the square footage that could be productive farmland. Through being made into a park, and no longer being used as an agricultural area, the ridge and furrow were never flattened; and Althorp today remains one of the rarest examples of a method of farming outmoded centuries ago, in its purest form.

The history of the Park is not as grand as that of the house, of course, but it has enjoyed its own special moments. In 1603 James VI of Scotland, whose dark portrait we have looked at in the Picture Gallery, came south to be crowned King James I of England. His queen, Anne of Denmark, stayed at Althorp with her son, Prince Henry, when en route to join her husband. The Sir John Spencer of the day proved to be a most thoughtful host, arranging for Ben Jonson to write a masque – then the most fashionable of aristocratic diversions – especially for the occasion.

The Park itself was the unadorned setting for the performance, as Agnes Strickland explains in her *Lives of the Queens of England*:

No painted canvas or coarse theatrical allusions accompanied this first masque of the mighty master. The scenery was the magnificent woodlands of an English park; instead of the boards, was the velvet green-sward under foot, and in the place of evil-smelling lamps, the glorious lights of heaven beamed down, through a midsummer night, on 'the Masque of the Fairies'. The queen, the heir of England, and the heir of Spencer, were themselves part of the 'dramatis personae' in this poetic welcome.

Ms Strickland seems to have had a severe attack of purple prose, but the masque was certainly appreciated by the Queen consort and her retinue. Sir John had arranged that, as soon as the royal party entered the Park, musicians would begin to play their wind instruments in welcome, with the performance proper starting before the coaches reached the mansion. Jonson's words were as flattering as the great pains taken by Sir John to entertain the new Queen. One of the principal characters, Queen Mab, opened with:

> Hail and welcome, fairest queen!
> Joy had never perfect been
> To the jays that haunt this green,
> Had they not this evening seen.

Prince Henry was presented with a dog, at which point proceedings took a slightly more macabre turn, when some unwilling participants in the evening's entertainment, a pair of deer, were let loose and, in Ben Jonson's words, 'were fortunately killed just as they were meant to be, in the sight of her majesty queen Anne'.

This all happening on a Saturday, and the Sunday being a day of rest, the rest of the masque was scheduled for the Monday. However, the royal party was effectively mobbed by loyal Midland folk who had flocked to Althorp to pay their respects. But Jonson had made his mark: he was the Queen's favoured author when she commissioned her own masques at court; and Sir John Spencer became First Baron Spencer, rewarded by James I for entertaining his wife so beautifully in the Park at Althorp. He was also reputed to have more ready money than anyone else in the kingdom, which would have earmarked him for a peerage in any case.

A generation later the Stuarts were again extravagantly entertained at Althorp. This time the royal guests were Charles I and Henrietta-Maria; the host was William, Second Baron Spencer. In honour of the visit, which was part of a royal progress through the Midlands, a new drawing room was constructed, the main hall was enlarged and improved, and a new stone staircase and new park gates were built outside.

The highpoint was a banquet, which cost £1,300. We know from the Althorp Household Accounts that the following was consumed that day: 8 pike; 14 perch; 20 bream; 20 tench; 6 barrels of oysters; 140 apricots; 6 boxes of cherries; 14 swans; 73 redshanks; 46 rabbits; 2 hogsheads of sherry; 1 hogshead of white wine; 2 firkins of cider; 40 hogsheads of beer; 24 dozen cakes; 40 pheasants; 26 partridges; 39 turkeys; 3 young peacocks; 2 lambs; 12 mallards; 7 teal; 6 young herons; 72 gulls; 300 tame pigeons; 500 wild pigeons; 4 storks; 100 quails; 14 dozen artichokes; 20 cauliflowers; 3,350 eggs; 560 lbs of butter; 39 dozen larks; 26 pigs; 13 veal calves; and, the ultimate excitement, potatoes! This was the first time that this great rarity – introduced to England in the previous reign – was ever served at Althorp. The humble spud; truly, food fit for a king . . .

The banquet involved so many guests that both indoors and outside were used; in the Park there were tents and bowers for those not able to be seated in Althorp itself. After the banquet all the guests gathered in the Park to watch equestrian displays from the hunt. There was also a chance to witness William's great passion, horse-racing. He had even introduced a racetrack inside the Park, which was unusual for the early seventeenth century, since horse-racing was only just regaining popularity.

By all accounts, King Charles I was very appreciative of his time at Althorp. He can have had no idea what events would overtake him when next he was a guest in the Park.

Across the valley from Althorp lies Holdenby, the remains of a palace that was originally built by Elizabeth I's adviser, Sir Christopher Hatton, in the sixteenth century. When Hatton was forced to accept that he had overreached himself, and acknowledge that he could not afford to pay for what was then a huge structure, he surrendered it to his monarch. From then on it became a royal palace for the Midlands.

In 1646, with Charles I's Royalist forces defeated by Cromwell's Parliamentarians in the English Civil War, the vanquished King retreated to Holdenby to await his fate. He lived a disciplined existence, devoting Sundays to private prayer, and reading for two or three hours a day the rest of the week, with chess a further diversion. For exercise, he would walk in the gardens at Holdenby; but there was no bowling green there, and so Charles would ride to Althorp for this, one of his favourite pastimes.

Evelyn records that the Althorp bowling green was next to 'a noble walk of elms towards the front of the house'. It was to be a historic spot, as recalled by a contemporary in the *Imprisonment of Charles at Holdenby*:

His Majesty being one afternoon at Bowles in the green at Althorpe, it was whispered among the Commissioners, who were then at bowls with the King, that a party of horse, obscurely headed, was marching towards Holmby [*sic*]; and for no good it was presumed, in regard neither the Commissioners nor Colonel Graves, who kept the guard at Holmby and was an officer in the army, nor the Commissioners' servants, had the least notice of it from any officer, or other correspondent in the army. Whereupon the King, so soon as he was acquainted with it, immediately left the green, and returned to Holmby.

From there he was taken to London, his trial, and his eventual execution at Whitehall.

There is no memorial to Charles I's visits, but there is to Sir Robert being made a baron. The Falconry, at the back of the Park, was built by the new Lord Spencer in 1613, the royal coat of arms on one side, the Spencer ones proudly displayed on another. Originally this was not for habitation, but for the ladies of the house to stand in, while the men showed off their prowess with their hawks. What is today three bedrooms at the front would then have been an open upper hall.

The Reverend Dibdin, George John's librarian, went up to the Falconry during repairs in 1818, where the workers had reported coming across some watercolours on the walls:

These subjects were too much mutilated by the workmen, occupied in the repairs, before I had an opportunity . . . of examining them fully; but sufficient

The Red Earl, accompanied by the Empress of Austria, riding to hounds by the Falconry.

was left to enable me to form a pretty accurate idea of the mode of hunting. In one part, nets were thrown over the bushes, and the foxes and hares were driven into a space, between them, and cudgels and hunting staves were liberally thrown at them. In another part, the dogs were yoked in couples; in another, they were giving chase to the stag. At a distance, was a full-dressed figure on horseback, in cap and feather, preceded by a sort of running foot-man, with a hunting spear slung across his shoulder; while, in the foreground, within some rails or paling, a man was concealed in the branches of a tree, shooting with a cross-bow at the animals below. The hawking or hunting stand – supported by six pillars – and having two stories of small glazed windows, is seen, above, to the left, while the spectators are looking on from the windows.

Over the centuries the Falconry was adapted, first becoming a house for the park warden, next for the gamekeeper, and then for the kennel-man who looked after the foxhounds; puppy shows were held here well

into the twentieth century. My grandfather then made the place the home for the resident land agent, a tradition which continued until, after a few short-term lettings, I made the Falconry my Althorp base. This it remained from the age of nineteen until I inherited the main house eight years later.

It is a wonderful home, its Gothic 'Hammer House of Horror' exterior belying its natural warmth and tranquillity. As with the Stables, so the Falconry benefits from being built out of the local ironstone; an unobtrusive red-brick extension being added in the late nineteenth century. The rooms inside are not large, the only sense of space being in the hall, with its generous stone staircase, worn in the middle by nearly four centuries of footsteps.

Although the Falconry is built on a natural viewing point, its location can also be explained by the proximity of the heronry. In the early seventeenth century this area contained pools and a brook, and was within easy flying distance of marshy areas to the north and north-east of the Park. These were all natural feeding grounds for herons.

At Althorp herons were regarded as a prized delicacy; the Household Books show that six herons were consumed at the banquet for Charles I in 1634. The youngest birds were considered the best to eat, because older birds tasted strongly of the fish that was the bulk of their diet. Indeed, it would not be too great an exaggeration to say that the young herons were harvested. The process would usually start in March, although an early spring would bring the matter forward: gamekeepers would wait until the parent herons were away from the nest fishing, and would shin up the trees with sacks, to capture the young, flightless birds. They would then be presented to a servant in the house known as the 'cram maid', whose job it was to look after the various birds that would be prepared for the table, capons and quails among them.

The diet for the herons was meal and bullocks' livers to obliterate any taste of fish the birds may already have acquired through their parents' feeding. This diet also had the advantage of fattening up the young birds quickly. Once they reached the required weight, the cram maid handed her charges over to the cooks for their master's table.

This was a seasonal delicacy, because once the birds were approaching maturity their flesh would be too overpowered with fishiness for the

The Falconry, built in 1613 in the same local ironstone as the Stables.

cram maid to be able to flush it through with her cleansing foods. Moreover, the birds would be strong enough to fly off, and could therefore not be captured or hand-reared with any ease.

Today, no herons nest at Althorp; even though they would, of course, be free from the demands of the dining room. They were here until 1993, but now they have moved to a pond two miles away. Some wondered if their exodus might have had something to do with Victoria and me keeping a herd of wild pigs in the wood, underneath their nesting place. However, a far more likely reason – especially as the pigs have long since gone and there has been no attempt by the birds to return – would seem to lie in the fact that the oak trees where the nests were built are reaching the end of their lives: the year before the herons left, seven nests fell to the ground as rotten or aged branches gave way.

The numbers of nests had been declining since the middle of the nineteenth century: in 1842, when John Charles sent three young herons from the nest of one of the gamekeepers to the Queen at Buckingham Palace, there were one hundred herons' nests at Althorp. By 1889 there were only ten. With luck, once the new plantation of trees at that end of the Park has established itself, they may return.

It is an irony, then, that the Falconry remains, long after the pursuit it was built to serve has ceased to be practised by the family in the Park, and after the main quarry has moved to other habitats. Down the years, this unpretentious, quirky building has delighted generations of my family with its charms: one of Georgiana Spencer's earliest recollections of Althorp, from the summer she spent there prior to her secret marriage, was of the Falconry:

I met with nothing in the park that pleased me more than the Keeper's house, for as I was riding about the park on a rising ground, I remarked a very pretty wood, which, when we came up to and rode round, I found there was a house and a little garden, placed so snug, that I saw nothing of it till we were quite close to it. There is a very pretty view from it, particularly of a castle, called Holdenby Castle; I could not help envying the people that lived in it . . .

I know how she felt: the Falconry has all the benefits of the Park, and none of the intrusions that accompany life in a great mansion.

Near by is another smaller house, full of character, the Dairy Cottage. This was built in 1786, originally with a thatched roof, by Lavinia, George John's wife. The couple had travelled abroad during 1785, and visited Versailles. There, they would have enjoyed Marie-Antoinette's folly, 'Le Hameau', which had its own dairy. Inside Dairy Cottage are the original Wedgwood tiles, as well as marble shelves; and further tiles, from Delft, surround the fireplace.

The two sixteenth-century stone pedestals have been mentioned earlier. Further ones were added around the Park in 1602, 1624, 1798, 1800 and 1901. They range from obelisk to plinth, and are a tradition I would love to add to one day; probably planting to commemorate the millennium. John Evelyn approved of the custom, at a time when only four of the stones were in existence, writing in his *Sylva*:

97

Dairy Cottage, built in 1786 by Lavinia, Countess Spencer.

. . . I have often wished, that Gentlemen were more curious of transmitting to Posterity, such Records, by noting the Years when they begin any considerable Plantation; that the Ages to come may have both the Satisfaction and Encouragement by more accurate and certain Calculations . . . But the only instance I know of the like in our own Country, is in the Park at Althorp in Northamptonshire, the magnificent Seat of the Right Hon. the Earl of Sunderland.

The gardens at Althorp are not its greatest feature, it has to be admitted. There is a watercolour in the Long Library of what the walled gardens at the top of the Park used to look like in the 1920s. That was the swansong for the Althorp gardens in terms of attempting anything ambitious; in the walls by the drying garden the four

An unsigned watercolour showing the walled gardens in 1926.

memorials to gardeners killed in the First World War mark the beginning of the end – after 1918 the ability of many great estates to employ at anything like the pre-1914 level was finished. The Red Earl may have had dozens of gardeners; by the time of my grandfather's death in 1975, there was one.

My father loved gardening, but Althorp was too large a canvas for him. He himself was only active in the garden of his house on the coast in Sussex. He had the formal gardens between the house and the Deer Park planted up with low-maintenance heather beds, so as not to stretch the solitary gardener too much, when he had all the lawns to tend, as well as making his daily weather report; still a custom at Althorp today.

The formal avenues at Althorp were supposedly designed by André Le Nôtre, for the Second Earl of Sunderland; this is probably true, although it is beyond doubt that Le Nôtre never actually visited Althorp – he must have designed the gardens while remaining in France. The next Spencer to make an impact on the gardens was the Red Earl. In 1860 he engaged W. M. Teulon to replace Holland's simple lawns that went all the way up to the edge of the house. This was probably at Charlotte's request, since she had spent a lot of her childhood at her grandparents' house at Ickworth, famous for its formal gardens.

Cypress trees were planted then. They never looked convincing in this quintessentially English setting, and they came to the end of their lives in 1998. Now they have gone, it is clear that Holland was right about the setting for his remodelled mansion: it looks incomparably finer without these foreign intruders standing next to it. The temptation is to fill in the garden beds too, and revert to lawn; perhaps even to parkland itself.

It has taken some time for me to feel the confidence to make changes at Althorp. After Grandfather died in 1975, and we moved to Northamptonshire, it was a difficult phase in all our lives; uprooted from our childhood haunts and friends, and marooned in the middle of a park the size of Monaco.

Raine allotted us rooms in the attics that had been thought adequate for junior housemaids in previous generations. My bedroom was eight feet by twelve which, when you look at a structure the size of Althorp, was not overly large. Diana and Sarah's rooms had the same proportions.

We were expected at mealtimes; breakfast was flexible, and lunch was meant to be at one o'clock. It rarely was, because Raine would usually have her breakfast in bed at eleven in the morning or so, and she would come down for lunch only when she was hungry again. Dinner in the evenings was formal: soup, meat, savoury and fruit (eaten with knives and forks!). All meals were served by the butler.

We all had our way of getting through the day. My passion was the Park, and I knew every inch of it. I was intrigued by the ice-houses at the back, where great blocks of ice were apparently stored for refrigeration. I was told that icebergs on the east coast of Canada would have bits carved off them, and then be transported back to great houses, such as Althorp, for storing in such underground chambers. My father had the main one sealed up after Bill Linford, who helped control the Estate's vermin with the gamekeepers, lost some of his terriers down one of them. He could hear them yapping in terror, as they scrambled to get a foothold out of there, before the noise stopped, the Jack Russells drowned.

The gamekeepers were always exciting to be with, and I went out with them whenever I could. Waiting for the Land Rover to sweep into the back yard at dawn is my memory of my summer holidays of 1977, when I was nervously anticipating starting at Eton, and wanted to make the very most of every hour of every day. It was really only then that I started to get to know the neighbourhood, the local farms and villages having been strangers to me until that point.

Back in the house, the staff were wonderful characters; I don't know if there is something about a life 'in service' which demands that you have an extraordinary personality, but Althorp has been blessed with many memorable people.

Edward John, Eighth Earl Spencer, in 1972, with his four children,
from left: Sarah, Charles, Jane and Diana.

The household staff in 1972, with Mr Pendrey the butler
in the middle row second from left and his wife in the front row far right,
with Mr Ward, the first nightwatchman, standing behind her.

Mrs Pendrey was housekeeper to my grandfather and to my father. The wife of the butler and a farmer's daughter from Norfolk, she was wonderfully warm, always screeching with laughter, her face glowing with plenty of make-up, her hair Spencer-red. The high point of her year was the first blast of winter, when the rats scurried into the cellars from the old rubbish tip. Mrs P would tie the bottom of her trousers tight with bailer twine, pick up her poker, and descend into the bowels of the house to do battle.

Later there was Jimmy, a five-foot Scot who had served in my father's regiment, the Scots' Greys, and worked for a year or two in the late seventies as footman. He spoke in a breathy hiss, and would sing regimental songs into my portable tape recorder. One day he came into the Tapestry Dining Room when my father was entertaining someone supposedly grand, carrying a decanter of claret. He tripped on the carpet, rolled around on the floor, somehow managing not to spill a drop, then jumped up, and retired from the room, all without a word. After he had failed to reappear, I was dispatched to find out if he was all right. He was in a dreadful state, shaking, and repeating to himself in a sort of mantra: 'I have been affronted, in front of the nobility. I have been affronted in front of the nobility ...' He then broke into a helpless, wheezing laugh, his ruddy face turning puce, as his wonderful sense of humour kicked in. Still, he would not return to the dining room that day, for he felt his pride had been dented; and because he feared he might start laughing again at the absurdity of it all.

Olga was altogether more bizarre. I think she was Portuguese, but she could have been South American. What was for sure was the fact that she was distinctly eccentric. On her afternoon off, she would pack everything she owned into her suitcase – including her alarm clock – arm herself with a walking stick, and then set off on foot for the front gate, and the bus to Northampton. The stick was to fend off the grazing bullocks, she said. Maybe she thought she was working at Woburn, and imagined they were altogether more exotic and menacing animals - buffalo? Anyway, she would stagger back into the Park in the evening, with her purchases from Northampton and all her worldly goods, unpack, and go back to work. This was a weekly performance that family and staff would watch with wonder.

These people were continuing a tradition that went way back. I can just remember Phyllis, as old as Grandfather, but still serving him the very basic food that he, as an active member of London's gentlemen's clubs, thought palatable. They had a love-hate relationship, Phyllis being one of the few people who genuinely was not frightened of him. Whenever there was a hint that she might be expected to perform above a level that she thought reasonable – and we are not talking Michelin stars here – she would quit her job until Grandfather had dropped his demands sufficiently. The end of the year used to be a favourite time for Phyllis to migrate back to Brington. 'Christmas wouldn't be Christmas,' Grandfather would say ruefully, 'without Phyllis's resignation.'

Of all the earls, I feel Grandfather must have experienced the greatest changes during his time in charge. This may be partly because, like the Red Earl's, his tenure of Althorp lasted in excess of half a century; but it was mostly because of the nature of the century in which he was adult: the twentieth. For Grandfather succeeded aged only thirty, eight years after the conclusion of the First World War, a

John Poyntz, Fifth Earl Spencer, with the future Seventh Earl as his pageboy at the coronation of King Edward VII in 1901.

104

conflict in which he was injured, left for dead, and survived only through a heroic rescue by a brother officer as he lay immobilized in no-man's land, a bullet through his knee.

By the time his grip on Althorp finally loosened in 1975, he had managed to keep the bulk of the collection together, and very definitely enriched the house, while simultaneously appreciating the place in a way that is sadly rare for someone born into his heritage. Grandfather was a true connoisseur, and Althorp was deeply fortunate to have him at the helm during the middle years of such a terribly turbulent century.

He had grown up the eldest son of Charles Robert, known as Bobby, the Red Earl's younger half-brother, and of Margaret, who died in childbirth in 1906. Margaret was a Baring, daughter of Lord Revel-

Charles Robert, Sixth Earl Spencer ('Bobby'), by Sir William Orpen.

stoke. Bobby was a celebrated dandy, whose natural hauteur William Orpen caught so brilliantly in his portrait, in the Saloon at Althorp.

On the Red Earl's death, Bobby was Lord Chamberlain, having already been created a peer in his own right: he was Lord Althorp, before becoming lord of Althorp. He had been a Member of Parliament, conscious that Althorp would one day be his, once it became clear the Red Earl and Charlotte were not able to have children. The Althorps and their six children had lived in Edwardian comfort at Dallington, then on the outskirts of Northampton, but were now firmly enveloped by it. The children were brought up to be musical – Margaret was a concert-standard violinist – and public-spirited.

After Margaret's death, Bobby was consumed by depression: the couple had been truly in love, as witnessed by his diaries, which I discovered in a bank vault, where they had been stored – unread – since his death in 1922. Each anniversary – of their meeting, of their engagement, of their marriage, of her death – was mournfully recorded in each subsequent year.

On the death of 'Uncle Spencer', as the children called the Red Earl, the widower and his three sons and three daughters settled into the more rarified atmosphere of the big house. It was a time of continued struggle, with Spencer House in London first being all but abandoned as a home by the family, and Bobby in despair about how he could keep even Althorp going at all. 'We're on the rocks!' he would say to the youngest of his six children, my great-aunt Margaret. And it must indeed have looked desperate, with the First World War apparently signifying the end of a way of life that no longer had a place in the twentieth century.

Commerce of any kind was not an option to someone like Bobby, and the idea of opening your house for money was considered deeply vulgar by most of the middle and upper classes. It seemed beyond hope that places such as Althorp could continue in the hands of their historic owners. The private palace had been destroyed as a concept as surely as the generation of young men who lay buried on the battlefields of Europe.

I have no doubt that Bobby would have sold Althorp if he could. The problem for him, and the blessing for future generations, was that there was no obvious buyer. There was also doubtless the feeling that he had

The Marlborough Room transformed into a dining room.

come into his inheritance by default, through the barrenness of his half-brother's marriage, and that Althorp was not really his to get rid of.

He did dabble with improvements, as much as his limited finances would allow. Two of the old libraries, the Raphael and the Domenchino, now stood as superfluous sitting rooms, both quite cramped, and adding nothing to the house. Bobby resolved to use them for something more useful, and had the connecting wall pulled down to form a large room, known as the Marlborough Room, after the fiery benefactor,

Sarah. It became the most formal of the various sitting rooms, a huge space that probably approximated to the area of the old Great Hall of the Tudor house; but intervening alterations had deprived it of symmetry. I always found it a difficult room, and changed it quite dramatically when I took over.

The electric power was also reorganized in 1910–11, the Spencers having worked out how best to use the newfangled invention rather more efficiently than had been the case when the electricity had first been installed by a bemused Red Earl a decade earlier. There was also the inspired use of black and white marble on the floor of the Wootton Hall, which we have already looked at. But, beyond these fiddlings, nothing much was done in the house; it would not have seemed worth it, for it was evident that the house would not last in Spencer hands for long.

As for the Great War itself, Canadian troops were billeted in the Sta-

Albert Edward John, later Seventh Earl Spencer, on his twenty-first birthday, from the *Northampton Independent*, 1913.

bles, and military manoeuvres were performed in the Park. These were not without their dangers, as the memorial to a cavalry trooper who broke his neck at this time testifies, by the Stue Pond.

By the time of Bobby's death in 1922, Althorp must have appeared an intolerable millstone. Grandfather came into the ownership of a property that thoroughly intrigued him, but which it seemed would inevitably be taken from him by the practical demands of the modern age. There was no unique library to sell, and the gems of the picture collection at that time were considered to be the great eighteenth-century portraits by Reynolds and Gainsborough. The problem for Grandfather lay in his love of his ancestors, for nearly all the twenty or so pictures that fell into this category were of his kinsmen. Just as the Third Earl could not dispose of his father's beloved books, so the Seventh would not sell his forefathers' images.

The comparative lack of funds of his father and half-uncle had left Althorp in a state only marginally less parlous than that of the mid eighteenth century, when emergency repairs were called for. Grandfather discovered that the roof was essentially rotten, and that the Wootton Hall wall facing on to the front courtyard was dangerously riven with damp.

Throughout his tenure of Althorp, he devoted whatever money he had to the maintenance of the building. By the time he died, he had peeled back the plaster and bricks to make them weatherproof again, and he had installed a solid roof, which still holds good today.

For such a gruff man – known behind his back as 'Jolly Jack' – Grandfather's private tastes were surprisingly refined; he was a Fellow of the Royal College of Needlework, and his handsome stitching still adorns firescreens

One of the tapestry chair coverings made by 'Jolly Jack'.

and cushions throughout the house. He was also a keen conservator, understanding the contents of Althorp probably rather better than he understood most people. His opening to the general public, a financial necessity from the 1950s onwards, was not a great success, as he really could not bear ignorance, and that, according to him, was what the general paying public displayed. The Georgian Society or other such specialist groups were always welcome; the average punter on a day trip was merely tolerated.

Grandfather tried very hard to do the right thing as earl, even getting his wife and children to lead a full-scale re-enactment in the Park of the Ben Jonson masque for Anne of Denmark. He was also an active supporter of the Northamptonshire Yeomanry, the local regiment which was formed by George John as a defence force against Napoleon's expected invasion. From the 1920s Grandfather had the duties of Lord Lieutenant of Northamptonshire, and consequently Althorp became a centre for the county's charitable work. If you read Grandfather's diaries, hardly a week goes by without the entry, 'Busy in the house', when he would be studying in the Muniment Room, or rearranging the display of china.

From what I gathered from my father, his childhood at the house, where he grew up with his sole sibling, older sister Anne, was not over-laden with happy memories; neither was it especially unhappy. It was just a small family of four living in a huge mansion, struggling to maintain the lifestyle that the house almost demanded of them. My father was very close to his mother, with his father a remote and undemonstrative presence in the background. From prep school and Eton, my father went straight into the war, and did not live on the Estate until he inherited Althorp over thirty years later.

During the Second World War many stately homes were damaged after being requisitioned by the War Office. The great rooms of history were turned over to the rough and tumble of military life, either as barracks, hospitals or training camps. Grandfather saw to it that Althorp House was none of these, and he managed to transfer the authorities' attention to the Stables, where troops were again billeted, leaving the house itself in a relatively undisturbed state.

When a local army officer came to pull down some of the iron railings around the house to help get his armoured car unstuck from thick mud, he was met with a full-on broadside from the peppery Seventh Earl, who made sure that no such liberties were taken again with parts of his inheritance. Thanks to Grandfather's intense love for the place, Althorp came through the war unscathed; although a Wellington bomber, which crashed up by the ice-house, killing all its young crew, nearly landed on the house, when spinning to earth, broken-winged and dying.

The eighteenth-century curled Spencer 'S's doorknobs.

Indeed, the war led to Althorp's greatest enrichment for over one hundred years, when Grandfather took the view that the pounding of London by German bombers made it imperative that as many objects as possible be moved from Spencer House to Northamptonshire; most of the furniture and other movables had already gone ahead over the previous twenty years, as the family abstained from using its desperately expensive London mansion.

It was then that the beautiful doors were taken down and reinstalled at Althorp, in such numbers that many of the doorways today have two doors, the curled Spencer 'S' adorning the doorknobs in all their eighteenth-century glory.

Even fireplaces were taken north to Althorp, away from the Blitz. The handsome ones in the Library, the Marlborough Room and the Picture Gallery originate from the state rooms at Spencer House, created by John Vardy. Even quite obscure guest rooms at Althorp were to benefit from these grand London designs. At the time, Grandfather was criticized for removing such focal parts of the rooms of Spencer House from their natural habitat, but he was vindicated when the Luftwaffe scored a direct hit with an incendiary bomb.

At the end of the War the financial position for owners of stately homes was far from promising. This was the time when Evelyn Waugh wrote *Brideshead Revisited*, as a mournful farewell to the era of great houses and their traditional owners, which now seemed certain to be at an end. Marchmain House, in the novel, stood for many mansions; and over the next two decades there was no shortage of large houses that were pulled down, or quitted, by families whose ancestors had lived there for generations.

Althorp survived in Spencer hands, although there was pruning: the back yard, with its myriad kitchens and storage rooms, was rationalized, half a dozen rooms being pulled down as Grandfather resolved to concentrate on preserving for as long as he could the core of the mansion.

It must have seemed quite hopeless. Grandfather explored in all seriousness the idea of giving the house to the National Trust, preferring to keep it and its contents intact, rather than fritter them away in a series of forced sales over many years. However, the National Trust had reached a stage where it no longer accepted gifts of houses on their own; it needed endowments with them, and Grandfather could not afford to go along that route.

Throughout the harsh tax regime of the 1950s, 60s and early 70s, Grandfather somehow struggled on. He lived such a thrifty life that, in 1972, when he wanted to plant a tree in the Park to mark his and his wife's golden anniversary, the Estate Office reported with embarrassment that there was no money with which to buy one. It was hastily arranged by Mr Sears, the Clerk of the Works, that some scrap should be sold from the Estate work yard to pay for this tiny expense. This was the ignominy that the owner of one of the greatest private art collections was reduced to.

Meanwhile, the upkeep and care of Althorp demanded authenticity, and Grandfather tried to meet this demand. The fact that he perceived his role as curator rather than owner is shown by his transforming the old 'Painter's Passage', Holland's corridor parallel to the South Drawing Room, into a museum-style display area for the family's china. Great banks of glass cases spanned the length of the passage, impinging on its proportions in an unsympathetic way. It was not that the china was not worthy of being displayed, so much as that by doing it in such a way, Grandfather was almost declaring, 'This part of Althorp will never be lived in again; so we may as well use it to show off the treasures in an orderly way.'

At the same time the Library was set up with druggets and ropes, enabling tourists to walk straight through what had in previous genera-

One of the fireplaces taken from Spencer House to Althorp to escape the Blitz.

tions been the principal sitting room for the family and its guests. Dust sheets covered the furniture when the house was closed.

The mansion was home to an elderly couple, living extremely modestly, with a minimal staff. But their age did have a minor benefit: Grandfather used his old age pension to pay for the re-covering of the set of eighteenth-century chairs in cool, light blue silk. It is a credit to Grandfather's matchless enthusiasm for Althorp that, when he died in June 1975, he left a house in excellent condition, the vast majority of its contents intact, all still in Spencer hands. Many of his peers failed to ride out the worst days of the punitive tax regime of the old-style socialists with anything like that level of success.

My father found the first three years of his time in charge at Althorp unexpectedly stressful and pleasure-free. Having had to wait until his early fifties to inherit, he discovered that the reality of trying to keep the whole operation afloat was rather more taxing than it had appeared to be, from behind his desk in his Norfolk study.

As he floundered, Raine, whom he married in 1976, took a firm grip of the situation; something my father felt simultaneously guilty about and grateful for. Sales were made to meet death duties. My father had long dreaded these taxes, as his scrapbooks show; he kept all the newspaper cuttings associated with this scourge of the wealthy, long before he had to deal with the taxes that came with his own father's death. He chronicled the inroads they made into inheritances old and new, the neatness of the cuttings' display unable to conceal the dread in his heart at how he would cope when his turn came.

When it did, the most valuable chattel to go was a double portrait by Van Dyck which used to hang above the Picture Gallery fireplace, *Lady Andover and Lady Thimbleby*, in spirit, the sister painting to *War and Peace*. My father told me later that he was in tears when it left the house for the National Gallery, for he knew its importance to the collection.

At this stage there was a definite feeling that Althorp, despite Grandfather's best efforts, might not be tenable for long. A new agent was brought in to shake up the traditional structure of the Estate, in an attempt to give it a viable future. This meant the premature demise of John Edwards, a decent and honest man, who had run the Estate for Grandfather in the manner in which he was expected to do. It is sad that he was not given time to show whether he could adapt to the new regime. Massive cuts were made in the staff, the forestry department shrinking to a total of two men, when once it had numbered nearer fifty.

At the same time as the estate was being radically restructured, the traditions of the house somehow survived. My father perpetuated the tradition of having a Christmas party for the staff, complete with carols, mince pies and mulled wine. All the family greeted the guests as they came into the Wootton Hall, and then the Saloon was the venue for the carols, before everyone decanted into the Great Dining Room for the refreshments. This annual fixture died out after Raine – never patient in those days with things Christian – experimented one year by changing the theme of the evening to Rodgers and Hammerstein-style hits. The general astonishment that greeted the lead singer as he swaggered into the Saloon, thumbs hooked into his belt, thumping out 'Old Man River', when everyone had been expecting a treble with a candle and cassock trilling the first verse of 'Once in Royal David's City', will live with me always.

On Christmas Day itself, we children would go to church at Brington, and then return to the house, where things would have been very precisely arranged, all the presents removed from under the twenty-foot Christmas tree in the Saloon and placed on a row of chairs in the Library; one chair per person. We had to take it in turns opening a present each, everyone else gathering around to watch. What it lacked in spontaneity, it made up for in embarrassment, as we had to demonstrate our most sincere gratitude in front of a large audience.

Raine once gave the redoubtable Mrs Pendrey a mink stole. I cannot remember her ever wearing it, but I am sure it was useful for scaring the hell out of the rats in the cellar, the smell of killer predator awakening all manner of instinctive fears in them before the poker even swung into action.

Later Christmases provided much happier memories, my father entertaining his grandchildren and their friends with parties they will probably remember for ever. Smartie Artie, a children's entertainer, would clown, tease and bewitch the children, all of whom were in fancy dress. When he had raised them to a fever of excitement and they could take no more, tea would be announced.

The Sunderland Room would have been transformed into a Christmas fairyland, with clockwork Santas, snowmen and angels all spinning and chiming in the candlelight. Each child had their place marked by a small cake, their name written large in icing. The only silence of the afternoon was the brief period between the children sitting down and their managing to fill their stomachs.

At the end of tea all the children were taken outside into the front courtyard, where, in unison, they hollered, 'Father Christmas! Father Christmas!', the steam of their breath billowing upwards, towards the tips of Holland's Corinthian pillars. The floodlights of the Stables would be on, and then, in silhouette against the ironstone, the form of Father Christmas and his donkey and trap could be made out, trotting along the drive to the front door of the Wootton Hall.

The children would be beside themselves with excitement by this stage, tugging at Santa's robes as he dismounted, and wanting to know what was in his sack. The answer was a generous present for each child, all carefully selected by my father at Hamleys on one of his seek-out-and-spend missions to London.

But that was not the end of it. Every child would be given a bag of chocolate money, which they could then 'spend' at the various stalls, manned by the house tour guides, each of which had a range of toys. I doubt whether there have ever been more successful parties at Althorp than those; certainly, they were the high point of my father's year.

Everything changed after September 1978. My father collapsed in the Estate Office from a massive stroke. He went over like a felled oak. 'I just felt I had to lie down,' he later recalled.

The coma he sank into seemed interminable, and we were told the devastating news by the doctors: he would definitely die. I was fourteen, and it looked as though I was on the point of having Althorp foisted on me at an age when most of my contemporaries were dealing with the demands of adolescence, rather than of heirlooms.

But my father's heart was strong, and he pulled through on a life support machine, despite pneumonia and kidney infections, saved by the

Edward John, Eighth Earl Spencer, with Raine, Countess of Dartmouth, at a dinner in 1977, a year before his stroke.

117

Edward John, Eighth Earl Spencer, with a magnum of Althorp Champagne in 1982.

fact that he did not smoke and rarely drank. Raine and my sister Sarah, separately, sat for hour after hour by his bedside. When he came out of hospital, it was clear that he was extremely fortunate, being left with only relatively minor problems with his balance and a perpetual short-ness of breath. He also had a different perspective on life, no doubt the result of his near-death experience: my father, for so long extremely cautious with money, began to enjoy his inheritance to the full, while handing over all responsibility for running Althorp to Raine.

All, that is, apart from his beloved wine cellar, where he would potter for hours, laying down new acquisitions and rejoicing in the jewels of his collection: the Château d'Yquem, the Petrus, the full range of 1924 ports. This was his true domain, where nobody else was welcome, and where he could spend hours undisturbed, in peace, at his own pace.

His other great joy was his wine shop, an extension of this cellar-cum-bunker, where he would spend many happy afternoons talking to visitors from around the world. He did not sell much wine, but that was irrelevant to him. He revelled in the diversity of the people who gravitated to his corner of the Stables to divulge their innermost problems to him. He would reappear in the late afternoon, in his stockman's coat, often unshaven – at other times partly shaven – with his flat cap askew, smiling merrily, and say, 'Good day today – two divorces and a hysterectomy!', before placing his meagre takings in the safe. I closed the wine shop down when I took over, out of respect for my father: it was so very much his hobby, his place, that it would have been wrong to perpetuate it after he was gone.

Across at the house, things were a little more frantic. An estimated £2 million was spent on redecorating Althorp in the 1980s. Much has been written about the question of taste with regard to these changes, and so I do not want to go into that here in any great detail. From the point of view of the family history, there were some real sadnesses, though.

During the Red Earl's time one of the house guests, Lord Charles Bruce, died at Althorp of smallpox. Because of the contagious nature of the disease, it was ordered that all materials in the room where he died should be incinerated. Charlotte Spencer, a relation by marriage of the dead man, set about replacing the curtains, bedspreads, tablecloths, even the fabric attached to the fire-guard, with hand-stitched patchwork on a beetroot-coloured silk background. The result was an outstanding memorial to the height of the Victorian age, as the Patchwork Bedroom captured so completely an era that had been of great importance to the house, but which had, elsewhere in Althorp, been eroded away by the intervening century.

The shiny, new, electric green velveteen placed on the walls of this room in the 1980s seemed somehow less special, less appropriate. But the option of going back to the authentic material at a later date was denied me, for the patchwork was simply thrown out; discarded; surplus to the requirements of a house whose contents must now sparkle and dazzle to have relevance.

Part of the patchwork was retrieved by the late Gervase Jackson-Stops, a senior and knowledgeable figure in the National Trust, and one of the great authorities on English country houses, who squirrelled it away at Petworth, handing it over to me when I inherited Althorp. Unbeknown to him, though, the storage arrangements were inadequate and, when I opened up the boxes where the patchwork had been for a decade, it had moulded and frayed beyond repair. The few scraps that survived can be seen on display in the Stables today, testimony to a woman who fully understood the importance of taste and style at Althorp, just as the electric green bears witness to one who, a century later, sadly did not.

The 1980s saw the exodus of the vast bulk of the religious paintings from Althorp; including, in fact, a scene from Exodus – Moses in the

Religious paintings were sold off in large numbers under Raine's management in the 1980s.

Sarah, Duchess of Marlborough's Dogs by George Stubbs.

bullrushes. The saddest loss was of individual portraits of four of the Apostles by Van Dyck. Other major casualties were *The Witches' Sabbath*, a gloriously macabre painting that had been one of the talking-points of guests at Spencer House in the nineteenth century; *Sarah, Duchess of Marlborough's Dogs* by Stubbs; and many dozens of other works, collected by 500 years of my family and now dispersed around the world, having sometimes been sent to London art dealers in laundry baskets from Althorp's back door, to guarantee the anonymity of the sale. Since my family was basically 'being taken to the cleaners' by the art world at the time, the laundry basket was perhaps the most appropriate mode of transport after all.

More mundane victims of this period, perhaps, were all the items in the cellars that had come from the other Spencer properties – Wimbledon, Harlestone, Wormleighton, Spencer House – fireplaces, baths, garden ornaments. These were cleared out by the lorryload, and sent to London, doubtless sold at a fraction of their value to middlemen, who then profited vastly from their resale. The shame was not simply financial, but also historical, as these last links with houses that had been family members' homes, some of them no longer even standing, were unceremoniously carted off to auction.

As the owner of a stately home in the late twentieth century, I appreciate it is common to have to sell the occasional item, usually out of extreme necessity, and almost always after taking the best advice from experts, artistic and financial. Sadly, the low prices being realized from the sales meant that yet more sales needed to be made. The international community of art dealers had a feeding frenzy at this stage of Althorp's history, cutting deals with one another so as to take turns in profiting from the apparently unstaunchable haemorrhage from the collection.

Perhaps there is something cyclical about such a process: just as 'good' marriages through the ages have been responsible for building up fortunes in prominent families, it seems that bad ones, with their attendant divorces and short-termist stepmothers, have made massive inroads into once secure inheritances. Between 1976 and 1992, I estimate that 20 per cent of the contents of Althorp were sold; which equates to a century of my family's 500 years of acquisitions disappearing, no doubt for good.

Immediately after my father's death, Raine appeared at Althorp armed with stickers to be stuck with prominence to all the things in the house that were hers. It was the grimmest tour of the house I had ever undertaken; reaching a crescendo at the end when Raine handed over the catalogues of chattels dating from Grandfather's time with the words: 'You'll find a lot of these things are missing. Still, you have more than most people, so don't complain.' She then wafted off, sixteen years of indiscriminate selling erased from her mind in a flash; oblivious to the end of the difference between an item's financial value and its heritage significance.

The events of 1976 to 1992 I have come to terms with now, and I have no longer any bitterness about them; merely great sadness. If there is one lesson I have learned, though, and which has been underlined during the writing of this book, it is that Althorp has undergone many peaks and troughs, and that it is as well not to be too judgemental until one has seen how wise one's own decisions have proved to be. It is important to see the humour in everything, of course, and that includes Raine's attempt to clad all the elegant Georgian rooms in the house in the ugliest imaginable double-glazing, the furniture cracking and tearing in protest as its annual fix of winter humidity was denied it;

Holland's Long Library, transformed during Raine's redecorating spree in the 1980s.

Holland's Long Library, which was only ever meant to be white, being stippled in glazed egg-yolk yellow; the noble pillars daubed in an attempt to make them look like malachite, but actually ending up resembling extremely long glasses of *crème de menthe frappée*. I must say, too, that it was some achievement to make the mighty Picture Gallery look mundane, by installing wall-to-wall oatmeal carpet: if I had not seen it, I would not have believed it possible.

It would be fair to say, then, that in 1992 I inherited Althorp in a state that none of my ancestors would have recognized. It was a very commercial affair, in that the house and grounds were open every day to the general public; but they came in very small numbers, as they did to the 'functions' of all kinds that were undertaken in the grander rooms. Through a failure to grasp even the most basic lessons of book-keeping, the house at this stage, with no money being spent on any of the necessary capital projects associated with historic houses, was running at a loss of over £400,000 per year.

In 1992 there was a massive house staff of fourteen, many of whom had had little to do in the previous years except form cliques and bicker.

There had been very much a divide-and-rule policy in the house, with three women taking it in turns to be her ladyship's senior figure in the hierarchy. The turnover of chauffeurs, maids, butlers and footmen was staggering, some not even lasting a week. Chefs rarely remained in favour for long, either, many of them I cannot even remember, but one I do because we bumped into each other in the linen room one day; not especially memorable, you might think, except for his attire. He was wearing absolutely nothing but a pair of white clogs. We both said 'good morning' and passed each other as though this was an entirely ordinary occurrence in an English stately home.

It became clear that things would need to change, and rapidly, if it was going to be viable to live at Althorp. Many of the house staff drifted away, aware that they would be superfluous to requirements, and we were left with a core of four. It was important to form a more professional set-up, so a clear division was made between the Estate Office, with its responsibility for the agriculture, cottages and timber; and the House Opening Office, with its aim of making the commercial activities in the Park walls a profitable business.

Out of realism it was necessary to face up to the fact that day visitors to the house would seemingly never balance the books, since Northamptonshire was a tourism no-man's land; whereas, conversely, Althorp's geographical location, half-way between London and Birmingham and a few miles from the M1, made it ideal for corporate entertainment. In my first couple of years at Althorp, the corporate business was looked after by well-meaning but under-qualified staff, who did their best, honestly and with charm. However, if we were ever going to challenge as a major player in this competitive market, it was evident that we would need the professional image that top clients rightly expect. Amazingly we achieved all our goals by the summer of 1997.

A series of blue-chip companies were returning to Althorp repeatedly, conscious of the fact that this was not simply a stately home dabbling in a little diversification, with snooty staff who did not really want to look after paying interlopers, but a business that fully understood their requirements, and a home which could provide a warm backdrop that is simply lacking in hotels and conference centres.

Day visitors were welcome for the sixty days a year for which we had, by agreement with the Capital Taxes Office, to be open; but the rest of the time we had marquees in the Park for dinners, fairs, concerts and classic car rallies; and presentations in the Red Earl's Great Dining Room, charity events in the Picture Gallery, a reception desk in the Wootton Hall and recitals in the Saloon.

By 1996 there was hardly a day between Easter and Christmas when there was not someone in the house or Park, preparing for, presenting, or cleaning up after an event. I remember a particularly surreal afternoon that summer when we were playing cricket on the pitch in the Park, to a live performance by José Carreras, as he warmed up his vocal chords on stage for that evening's concert. Sadly, not even his efforts could lift my team's play above the truly abysmal, but it was magical music to drop catches to.

It was usually extremely busy with lorries shuttling to and from the back door with groceries and wine, chairs and tables, and all the paraphernalia required for corporate events. The Park took quite a pounding whenever it was wet, and I always recalled my father's advice to remember what happened at Sandringham, when a caravan rally in a downpour resulted in the long-term scarring of the park there, when we were children. To date, fortunately, nothing as catastrophic as that has happened; testimony to the springy turf that Sir John Spencer chose as his grazing land back in 1486.

My general aim had always been to have events that are appropriate to Althorp. By that I do not mean on some appalling, snobbish level; but that only things that somehow seemed to fit the feel of the place were allowed. The Rolls-Royce Enthusiasts' Club staged their annual rally here, and it was wonderful to see 1,300 beautiful cars of all vintages spread across the Park, on parade for fellow members of the Club and their guests. Similarly, a huge cross-section of rural people come to Althorp for the annual Falconry Fair, when the ancient pursuit that has such a history in the grounds returns for a weekend.

BT twice held three-week-long forums in the house, with Althorp hosting their guests from all sectors of their clientele. The contrast between the high-tech nature of their products and the classical beauty of the rooms made for a perfect blend.

I have put the business side of things on hold for now, as we have all been dealing with the far more weighty matter of preparing Althorp for day visitors, keen to pay their respects to Diana.

When I inherited Althorp, I had no pretensions as to any great knowledge of art or architectural history, and I really did not know the house itself at all well, having been an infrequent visitor in early childhood, and then away at boarding school, university and working in London. Indeed, as a schoolboy, I spent half my holidays with my mother in Scotland, so I had probably only spent three or four hundred nights of my life at Althorp by the age of twenty-seven.

I was quite overawed by the prospect of running the house, but the dozens of family portraits on the walls made this ultimately a friendly place, somewhere I knew I belonged, and to which I could contribute. There was a deep sense of security in seeing all the preceding generations gathered round in encouragement.

Older friends suggested experts who might come to advise me on how to refurbish the place – to return to some feeling of authenticity, such as had been present in Grandfather's time, while also making it possible for a young family – Victoria and I had our twin second and third daughters soon after my father's death – to live there.

I remember a fascinating day spent with John Hardy from Christie's, who understood all the motifs in the Wootton Hall and interpreted the symbolism for me, while also explaining what the furniture's qualities were. Then there was John Cornforth, a regular visitor to Althorp when Grandfather was here, with a deep love for the authentic, who winced every time he walked into a room that was all candyfloss pink, or flock-wallpapered like a balti house, or weighed down with inappropriate, busy patterns. 'I'm sorry,' he concluded, 'but I simply don't see where you can begin; it's almost beyond hope.'

He was echoing my deepest fears. The shrieking over-gilding on the Spencer House furniture; what could possibly be done to make it at least bearable? The darkness of the Saloon, which had been designed to look clean and simple with the natural light from the skylights; was

Charles Edward Maurice, Ninth Earl Spencer, by Graham Jones.

The South Drawing Room in the 1980s, gilded to within an inch of its life.

there anything that could blow away its drabness? The carpeting every-
where, which made everything so uniform, so very unappealing ... It
went on and on.

At the same time there were very definite problems that ran deeper
than mere decorative matters: the plumbing was near the end of its life
after decades of faithful service, the pipes furred up with sediment. The
contents were dramatically under-insured, while the burglar alarms
and smoke detectors were hopelessly outmoded. The window frames
had been denied basic maintenance for over a decade and were warped
and flaking, rotting and unusable. At least the roof was in good order,
thanks to Grandfather's efforts in the 50s, when he had dealt with the
rot; and to John Love, the plumber's, unfailing attention in the interim,
making sure that drains were always unblocked, slipped tiles replaced.
The roof to the old Servants' Hall in the back yard was the only weak
link, concertinaed with neglect.

The first thing was to make the place habitable for us as a couple
with our children. Our bedroom was transformed, and the Nursery
was made practical. The main passage in the private wing and the

staircase up to the top floor from there were returned to an approximation of the Edwardian green they had been dressed in before the effrontery of the 80s. Throughout the house, the beautiful floorboards were liberated from their wall-to-wall carpeting, soaking up huge quantities of wax, so long denied them. It was wonderful to see the rooms regain their dignity, as this very simple process gave them back their true proportions.

The Celestial Globe – one of a pair of George II library globes.

The celestial and terrestrial globes on which John Charles, as a young boy, had had his first geography lessons 200 years earlier, were returned from the Picture Gallery to the Library, their proper home. Meanwhile, I used the heavy, uncomplicated oak panelling of the Picture Gallery to absorb the worst excesses of the overgilded Spencer House furniture: this was a room secure enough in its own masculine identity to render the embarrassing tartiness of these chairs and sofas insignificant.

The Chapel, transformed in the 80s into a humble junk room, was

The Chapel, March 1982, used as a storeroom.

restored to its proper function. A house that had boasted scores of religious paintings twenty years earlier, could muster only eight now; just enough to cover the walls. The French grey of the walls was washed down rather than repainted, and the beautiful stained glass windows, brought from Wormleighton Manor in the nineteenth century, were polished anew. Pews were found in outbuildings, others were borrowed from near-by churches, and the old priest from Maidwell, where I had been a schoolboy, managed to locate a small but pretty organ, which was added to the room.

A stained glass window in the Chapel. The armorial glass dates from 1588 and came from Wormleighton Manor, the original Spencer family residence.

The Tribute Money by Guercino, which hangs in the Chapel at Althorp.

The Chapel had been a busy room until Grandfather's time. George John and Frederick had been intensely religious men, both preaching there. And my great-grandfather, Bobby, the Sixth Earl Spencer, had continued the practice of having a daily service there; sometimes two. The family would sit, with the staff standing at the back, then. Grandfather had used it occasionally as well, inviting clerical friends to take the service. It was very gratifying to see the place alive again. Three of my children were christened in this room, and it is still used for Christmas, Easter and Harvest Thanksgiving services when the family is at Althorp.

A member of the family, the Honourable George Spencer, has his portrait above the door leading into the Chapel. I have put him there, while the possibility of his being made a saint is resolved: he is a fair way towards this goal, on the strength of his devotion to the very poor, which saw him turn his back on his privileged position, as a gentleman-priest in the Anglican church, and brother of the Third and Fourth Earls, to live as a member of the devout Passionist Order, his

The Honourable George Spencer – English School 1890.

only possessions a cloak, a staff and a pair of sandals. If he is canonized, he will be promoted to a place in the Chapel; I have promised him that . . .

The Long Library had its busy lozenge carpet rolled back and its natural colour restored: there are thirteen different shades of white in the room, with the leather-bound volumes showing their richly coloured spines off against a crisp, neutral backdrop, as Holland always intended. It briefly became my study; with sweeping views of the Deer Park, it was wonderful to use it for more than just a sitting room when we had

One of the pair of torchères from Spencer House
that now reside either side of the fireplace in the Saloon.

lots of guests. But it is too isolated from the private wing, and walking through people who were holding corporate events there was disturbing and embarrassing for all concerned.

The Saloon had been covered in a dreary rust wallpaper, with an overactive russet pattern closing the room in on itself. It was so dark in there that massive candelabra had been placed at strategic points up the staircase, looking ugly and intrusive, springing up out of the wooden banisters with surprised expressions, wondering what they had

done wrong to be treated so inappropriately. It was clear these had to come down again, which made the brightening of the area by some other means of the utmost urgency.

Again, Holland's love of white was the authentic and practical solution; it is a lesson I learned during this time that authenticity invariably equals good taste. The candelabra were not missed, and the room recaptured its majestic simplicity, the family portraits around the higher level, an assortment of royals, generals and courtiers below. It was good to see them re-emerge from the shadows.

Most recently, in June 1998, the Garden Lobby behind the Saloon staircase – in previous generations the bedroom to the lady of the house – was turned into a China Museum. The shelves that had so spoilt the lines of 'Painter's Passage' were reused, stacked one on top of the other in places, and all the best pieces of a highly diverse collection – Meissen, Sèvres, Kangxi, Chelsea, Derby – are now on show, much happier in their purpose-designed space than as sprawling interlopers, slouched against the Passage wall. The most interesting display is of a beautiful, dark blue chocolate service that was made at Meissen for

Covered bowl and stand, Meissen porcelain, *c.* 1745.

135

The China Museum, formerly the Garden Lobby.

A unique Sèvres tobacco pot with attached spoon.

Meissen bowl, *c.* 1745.

Marie-Antoinette – who was a friend, until her execution, of George John's sister, Lady Harriet Spencer, later Countess of Bessborough.

There is also another piece that shares both royal connections and rarity value. Queen Mary, George V's wife, was a guest whose visits the stately-home owners of Britain used to anticipate with mixed emotions. She had an eye for fine objects, and a very definite way of transmitting what was particularly intriguing to that eye; to the extent that her hosts would invariably feel duty-bound to offer her the object of her admiration as a gift. These were not offers that she was in the habit of turning down.

When she came to stay at Althorp with the King in 1913, my great-grandfather must have feared that a depletion of the collection was imminent. Imagine how surprised he must have been when the Queen actually gave him a china pot for his collection, rather than requisition one. It is here at Althorp today, its provenance perhaps unique.

My favourite items in the China Museum are the late seventeenth-century *tulipières*, special vases designed to hold individual stems of tulips. These flowers were highly fashionable after the accession of the

A pair of late seventeenth-century *tulipières*.

Painters' Passage.

Dutchman William of Orange to the English throne, but they were rare enough to be reputedly worth more than their weight in gold. It was therefore important to present one's few tulips with the greatest care; hence the *tulipière*.

The moving of the china has freed up the area where it used to be, Painters' Passage, allowing it to be returned to its old function of displaying self-portraits. I have always found these among the more fascinating art forms, revealing how artists have seen themselves. The one of

Sir Joshua Reynolds, self-portrait.

Sofonisba Anguisciola, self-portrait.

Reynolds is very good, as you would expect; but the most captivating is by Sofonisba Anguisciola.

Sofonisba was one of six talented sisters, all of whom were artistic. Living from 1527 until 1625, she is remarkable not only for her longevity, but also for being one of the first successful women artists in Europe. There are several self-portraits by her, but this one, three-quarter length, in front of a clavichord – similar to a harpsichord – with her nurse behind her, is special because of the contrasting dress, age and style of the two women it features. It is one of the most interesting works in the collection; and, again, it is thanks to Sarah Marlborough that it is at Althorp. She bought it for £140 at Earl Cadogan's sale in 1726.

There are not, at present, enough self-portraits to cover the length of the passage, so works portraying other artistic figures – the author, Molière; the actor, Garrick – substitute in the meantime. I have bought one picture for this passage, but will have to find more.

The labyrinthine attics had been treasure troves during Grand-father's time, each room heaving with furniture and paintings for which there was no space in the house proper. They had been trawled through for anything of value many times in the 80s, so there was nothing much left there by 1992. Still, something needed to be done with them, and Victoria chose some wonderful, old-fashioned paints from the National Trust range to complement their 'upstairs, downstairs' feel. Pastel and bold dark shades gave these rooms, so long devoid of the servants they originally housed, meaning again, as they became overflow guest rooms; and, latterly, important storage spaces, all meticulously looked after by the tireless Ian, the second successive male housekeeper.

The old Servants' Hall, where the long-gone occupants of the attics would have eaten, the senior staff being served by their lowlier col-leagues, was suffering from neglect so I had its roof repaired and the tiles straightened out. I gave it a new function as a totally informal room, with a huge table down the middle and a durable carpet, where we could all relax, friends, family, children, whatever the weather was like outside. During cricket matches or winter weekends, it's the perfect place for meals with all age groups joining in together, not frightened of spilling anything, or knocking over something of value. My children have learned to master the circuit round the refectory table to perfec-tion at the wheels of their Toys'R Us cars, missing the corners by millimetres as they thunder past in pursuit of one another.

My father had sold the family's records to the British Library in the 80s, leaving the Muniment Room empty. This area was then converted into 'the Steward's Room Flat', and it was advertised in Japan as the perfect place for newlyweds to honeymoon. Given that it overlooked

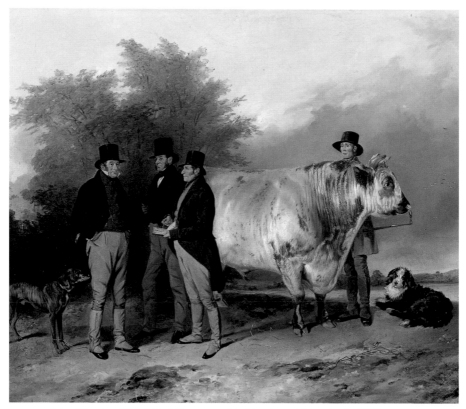

John Charles, Third Earl Spencer, with friends and his prize bull Wiseton,
by Richard Ansdell, 1843.

the bins and the oil tank in the backyard, it failed to capture too large
a market. (My father's other unsuccessful venture at this time was a
trout farm, next to the heronry . . .) However, it had the great advantage of being in the same section of the house as the traditional private
quarters of the family. The young children, who would usually have
been far away from their parents and near the Nursery, could therefore
be brought very close to us by some minor modifications to these
rooms. Our daughters insisted on keeping one of the bathrooms as a
cacophony of clashing pinks, as it had been decorated, because they
thought it a perfect place for their Barbies to bath with them; so a
complete overhaul was fortunately not required.

Displaced from this end of the house at this point were half a dozen
paintings of the prize bulls of John Charles, the thrifty Third Earl,
including a magnificent one of his champion, *The Durham Ox*. I later
found a further twenty-two of these pictures, each showing an individ-

Ranunculus by Richard Ansdell.

An Ox by Wiseton by Richard Ansdell, 1839.

An Ox by Jeremy by William Henry Davis.

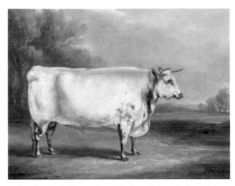

An Ox by Wiseton by Richard Ansdell, 1838.

Orontes by Richard Ansdell.

ual square-built bull. After some research I realized that these were the Third Earl's main contribution to the art collection of the house. Indeed, apart from some portraits of himself, there was nothing of note from his tenure.

When I reorganized the Sunderland Room, a large sitting room on the ground floor which had 150 years earlier been the Earl's Bedroom, I decided to dedicate it to the memory of a modest but able man who had done so much for Althorp, and whose peculiar passion could be commemorated through hanging the bull paintings en masse. Elsewhere in the room, the medals these beasts won for him are encased and on display.

Next to the Sunderland was the Marlborough Room which, I have already explained, never felt satisfactory to me as a large drawing room. The reasons are clear: it was never meant to be one room, and the pillars which should be in the middle, but most definitely are not, accentuate the fact that the proportions of it are wrong. Both Grandfather and Raine had assembled furniture around the two fireplaces, hoping by doing so to blur this problem. In fact, I think they only succeeded in accentuating the unhappy proportions of the space.

The solution was to transform this problem drawing room into a glorious dining room, where the length of the table pulled both parts of the space into one cohesive whole. The dining room table, with its fifty-four chairs designed by Seddon, came from the Great Dining Room, the Red Earl's addition to the side of the house.

This was hardly the work of a genius, I appreciate, but it shows how my early fears that it would be impossible ever to make any impression on Althorp were wrong: even the simplest idea can transform the feel of a place which, despite its scale, is a series of rooms, as in any other house; and, as in any other case, the occupant is free to impose his tastes. Roll up a carpet, move a table, and things start to change. This could not be more true than in the whole underrated art of picture-hanging.

I was lucky, after an unsatisfactory experience with an interior designer, to be approached by Edward Bulmer, who had helped Lord Rothschild to resurrect the splendours of the interiors of Spencer House in the 80s. Edward wrote out of the blue to offer his services, and since then he has transformed the inside of the house by first getting to

The Marlborough Room as a drawing room.

know each painting, then cataloguing it and finally hanging it in an intelligent, appropriate way. It does not sound an important consideration, but it is.

Perhaps the most notable collection of portraits by one artist at Althorp is that of Sir Joshua Reynolds, a close friend of the family, who painted most of its members during his lifetime. These are the very essence of eighteenth-century portraiture, complementing the house so well that how best to display them needed careful thought. A hundred or so years ago there had been a tendency to hang them all together, in what is now the South Drawing Room. Some have returned there, along with other works, by Gainsborough and Battoni, to form a wonderfully rich and compact collection; bold and striking images, that contrast with the collection of exquisite miniatures in alcoves in the recesses of the room, taken from the bank vault to be enjoyed, rather than hoarded away out of sight.

The room between the South Drawing Room and the Library was known in the 80s as the Rubens Room. It was a dead space: desperately uncomfortable furniture, and Rubens's imposing portraits of several unattractive Habsburgs, against a tightly patterned silver silk, making it anything but welcoming. This is now brought alive by a busy hang of thirty-two paintings with a predominantly sporting theme, from

Lady Anne Bingham,
by Sir Joshua Reynolds.

Lady Lavinia Bingham,
by Sir Joshua Reynolds 1782.

147

Georgiana, Countess Spencer, with her daughter Lady Georgiana,
later Duchess of Devonshire, by Sir Joshua Reynolds.

Lady Georgiana Spencer, later Duchess of Devonshire,
by Sir Thomas Gainsborough, *c.* 1760.

148

Scape Flood by George Stubbs.

Stubbs's racehorses to Wells's glorious evocation of the Red Earl and
Charlotte resting while watching a rifle shoot on Wimbledon Common.
Paintings of Althorp in the seventeenth century, resplendent in red
brick, formal gardens to one side; and of Spencer House, a hundred
years later, with Buckingham Palace in its previous guise – also red
brick – add to the sense of continuity and development that are the
family's twin themes.

The Billiard Room.

It is now the Billiard Room – so called because pride of place goes to the old billiard table, found in a hundred pieces in the Stables six years ago, chewed by rats and with a damaged slate. It is now fully restored, and helps give an accessible feel to all three rooms of 'the Holland Suite'.

The main room of the three is Holland's greatest contribution to Althorp: the Long Library. It is here that the most celebrated of the remaining Reynoldses and other prime eighteenth-century portraits are arranged in a family group. In the centre, full-length, is John

John Charles, later Third Earl Spencer, aged four, by Sir Joshua Reynolds.

Charles, dressed as a young page-boy, with a turquoise sash – the model for the page-boys' outfits at both my parents' and my own marriages. It is a portrait that fully captures the softness of its subject; John Charles being, incidentally, probably the only person who sat for Reynolds and, sixty years later, for a photographic portrait as well.

Either side is a Gainsborough of Georgiana, the First Countess; and portraits of George John – reading, of course – of his wife, Lavinia, and of two of their younger sons, Admiral Sir Robert Spencer and Admiral Frederick Spencer, later Fourth Earl. It all represents a great improvement over the series of fine but brittle gilded mirrors, and the single Guercino painting, *The Tribute Money*, that previously struggled to hold together such a great room.

In virtually every room, Edward Bulmer has redesigned the hang of the pictures. It has been an Estate effort, though, with all members of staff at some stage being called in to help move the paintings around. One day, I have no doubt, my son Louis will move them all back again . . .

Georgiana Poyntz, Countess Spencer, by Sir Thomas Gainsborough.

S uch was her appeal that everyone remembers the moment they heard of Diana's death. My memories are of telephone calls in the middle of the night, one of which confirmed the very worst: the car crash had been fatal.

It soon became clear that practicalities would have to be dealt with. While arrangements for the funeral started, so did the question of where she should be buried.

For nearly five centuries members of the family had been placed in the chapel in St Mary's, Brington. Most recently my grandparents and my father had been buried there; the sealed entrance chiselled open, before being cemented shut again. In 1992, when my sisters and I placed the urn with our father's ashes down in the vault, I had said to the three of them, 'Do you realize, one of us is probably going to have to go through this sort of thing with the other three of us?' It seemed that the first of those occasions had arrived, all too soon.

Yet, just as plans were being made to place Diana with her ancestors, a message came from London that she had specifically requested in her will that her remains be buried in a coffin, rather than cremated. This worried me enormously, because ventilation would be needed; and with ventilation necessarily came some sort of access to the vault. All the ancestral bodies had been tidied up and cremated by Grandfather in the 50s, and the last three burials had been of ashes.

There was also the question of the effect on Brington. The village was already being overrun by tourists and the media, since it was anticipated that this would be the place where Diana would be laid to rest. Put simply, it was doubtful that the village could cope.

These were the darkest of days, when family grief was all but matched by the devastation of a nation that had witnessed the demise of someone who had seemed as far removed from death as it was possible to be.

The Spencer Chapel at St Mary's, Great Brington.

Anyone who has experienced the death of a close relative will know that insomnia is one of the symptoms of intense grief. It was during such a spell of listless wakefulness that I realized that we would have to bring Diana inside the Park, in order to protect her – and Brington – as best we could. From there, it was a short step to deciding that the island in the Round Oval would be the best place for her to be buried. She loved water: it was her element. There was also the fact that the water would act as a buffer against the interventions of the insane and ghoulish, the thick mud presenting a further line of defence. We all agreed that, with its beauty and tranquillity, this was the place for Diana to be.

The Round Oval and Summer House before their redesign.

Six days after the burial, at which the Princess of Wales' Regiment had performed so magnificently, a meeting took place in the Great Room at Althorp. Present were my two managers, the police, the highway authorities, local councillors and myself. The agenda was simple: now we had seen the thousands of people bringing their floral tributes to the gates of the Park, how were we to cope with the invasion of people who would descend on Althorp and its environs, once we opened for sixty days per year, as we are legally obliged to do?

One senior police officer pointed out that Princess Grace of Monaco's grave apparently attracts 10,000 visitors a day during the summer. It was clear, given Diana's even greater global appeal, that we could be facing several times that number each day we were open; and it was obvious we could not cope with that – not the Estate, not the roads approaching the area, not Northamptonshire.

Over the next weeks a plan was formulated: we would open for sixty days, as required; we would make each day's ticket allocation 2,500, so preserving the dignity of Althorp; these tickets would be available only in advance, and it would be made clear that nobody arriving at Althorp without a ticket would have a chance of entry; all profits would be handed over to Diana's Memorial Fund; an exhibition would be created in the Stables to celebrate Diana's life and mark the impact of her death. In September 1998, when the gates of the Park closed again, we would re-evaluate and decide what to do in future years.

It was now important to put together a team to deal with the plans – plans that had to be implemented by 1 July, the date that we had agreed with the government prior to Diana's death would be our first day of opening. It was the date of Diana's birth. Similarly, by a strange coincidence, we were committed to be open for sixty days from then, which took us close to the date of her very premature death: 31 August.

I had clear instructions for everyone who was on the project:

Charles Spencer lays flowers on the island at Althorp where his sister is buried.

'Everything has to be beyond reproach; and we have to take Althorp out of the stratosphere of the conventional English stately home.' Both objectives were in honour of Diana; both were to be achieved via the best judgement of ourselves – certainly not via the howlings of the media who, furious that the goose that laid the golden eggs was no longer there to help their circulation figures, had decided to whip up endless accusations and controversies about my family's plans at Althorp, in an attempt to create 'reader-interest'. It seems an unduly cruel and hurtful campaign to have undertaken against a grieving family.

David Horton-Fawkes, a wise and spiritual man, as well as a highly professional one, was in charge of the project. He had run the corporate business in the house and Park previously, and before that had a distinguished record in hotel management. I knew our plans could not be in better hands. What is more, I knew he would see everything was finished on time which, given the fact that we had only three and a half months to get everything in order once planning permission was granted, was a major consideration.

Having Frances Mossman on the project was also a comfort. She had been a prime creative force behind the entrepreneur George Davies in the 80s. She was also a senior adviser to the National Trust, and had undoubted artistic flair, as shown by her post as lecturer at St Martin's School of Art. To Frances went the task of stocking a shop which was tasteful and which used neither the name nor image of Diana to sell its wares. The results are among the most innovative and attractive range of souvenirs and gifts of any shopping outlet at a tourist site. Frances and her business partner, Fiona Sale, focused on three ranges, inspired by Althorp, by Diana's love of natural products, and by her love of children, respectively.

The latter was the most appealing of the three. Among the tens of thousands of condolences we received at Althorp from children, the cards of Little Heath Primary School, Potters Bar, stood out because of their vibrancy and charm. We invited the school to bring the pupils over for a tour of the house to see what we were planning and to establish if they were interested in allowing us to base a range of goods on their designs. They were; and the resulting products are wonderful additions to the shop's stock, their attractiveness complemented by their freshness.

But Frances's involvement did not end there: she suggested others who might be able to play a pivotal role in making Althorp relevant and meaningful, never losing any of her impetus, even when being pursued and door-stepped by tabloids, eager to find controversy where there was none.

We knew Althorp was classical and weighty. We knew Diana was modern and inspirational. The plan was to fuse the various elements to make something appropriate, something worthy of her contribution to people's lives. It had to be tasteful and elegant, thought-provoking and satisfying; ultimately, it had to show why she became special to so many, in her seventeen years on the world stage.

The exhibition, in Morris's Stable Block, needed to be designed by someone who understood Diana's modern qualities, while appreciating the beauty of the eighteenth-century building in which he or she was to work. Rasshied Din had the right approach, according to Frances. His work for Red or Dead, Ralph Lauren and Dr Marten had the appropriate sense of style, while his commissions for W. H. Smith and the British Airports Authority, although perhaps lacking glamour, showed how seriously he was to be taken as a top-flight designer.

Rasshied's trademarks are clean, simple lines, and clever use of light and space. He has produced six rooms out of the former carriage houses and stabling areas, in which Diana's life and death are set in context. In other parts of the Stables, he has transformed the old-style tea room into a modern, sweeping restaurant, using many of the old features of the time when this was a place for horses, and making it suitable for the most discerning of visitors.

Across the yard, he has given Frances the most modern of shops, with a handsome slate counter and innovative display areas. Everything is crisply presented, relevant and clean-cut. We have kept the shop small, because commerce is not the point of the exhibition, or of its attendant services; serving the public is.

It is a truism that the public really do notice the standard of loo provided for them at venues such at Althorp, so it was decided not to stint on making them of the highest quality: everyone appreciated that many people would see their day at Althorp almost as part of a pilgrimage on Diana's behalf, so portaloos in the corner of a field would clearly be inappropriate. Thirty-three tonnes of Northamptonshire ironstone, as near as possible to the material used by Morris two and a half centuries ago, have been used on the construction of the loos and the improvements to the Stables. The doors and partitions of the cubicles are oak, the dominant tree of the Park. To give an idea of the number of visitors that are expected, the cess pool is 165,000 litres – the same size as three chemical tankers – and we are informed that it will have to be emptied weekly when Althorp is open.

The scale of works has been huge. Barry, the foreman from Jesse Mead, has been a source of optimism and cheerfulness throughout the building: 'I haven't been late on a project yet in my career; and I'm bloody well not going to make this the first time!' was his reassuring view of things. On average he has had 160 men per day working at Althorp. To put that into perspective, the caterer at the on-site burger bar for the men claims to have served them 30,000 bacon rolls between March and the end of June.

It has not all been bricks and mortar, though. The Stables being such an important listed building, the local planning officers have rightly insisted that everything be done to the highest standard: the plaster has been packed with real horse hair – two large horses' worth; the old, pitted floorboards have merely been covered with a new layer of oak, rather than being ripped out; the two staircases, butchered and hacked around in the 80s, have been put back as they were when this building was at its zenith. Most dramatically, the front doors in the two forward towers, overlooking the front lawn, have been put back, the stone that had been in their place removed, giving the Stables back its proper features for the first time this century.

All this primarily to set off the exhibition to its best effect. The business of making the exhibition relevant and fulfilling fell to Catherine McDermott, another contact of Frances Mossman's, an experienced curator who could juggle the expectations of the public with her expertise in fashion, and the confines of the spaces on offer for displaying the various items.

It was decided to break the exhibition down into seven rooms, each with its own theme. The first is called 'Spencer Women'. If there was something we could do at Althorp, which nobody else possibly could, it was to set Diana in context. So here we have Sarah, Duchess of Marlborough, with some of her jewellery, and her greatest portrait, by Sir

Godfrey Kneller; here also, by Sir Thomas Gainsborough, Georgiana Spencer, later Duchess of Devonshire, and one of the most glamorous figures in eighteenth-century England, who used to cause similar reactions among the people of London during her public appearances, as Diana did, 200 years on; also Lavinia, Second Countess Spencer by Sir Joshua Reynolds, another independent, ground-breaking woman, friend of Nelson and Sir Joshua Reynolds, who painted this portrait; fourthly, Charlotte, the Red Earl's wife, and the hand behind the Patchwork Bedroom, who was considered one of the great beauties of nineteenth-century England; and then

Cynthia Hamilton, wife of the Seventh Earl Spencer, by John Singer Sargent.

Grandmother, in a cool sketch by John Singer Sargent, a lady who, a quarter of a century after her death, is still remembered with love by the people of the county for her charitable works – to the extent that they named the hospice in Northampton after her.

To the world at large, Lady Diana Spencer first came into prominence in 1980 or 1981; but the point is she did not come from nowhere. By showing the themes she was continuing, it is easier to make sense of her later contributions. She was always proud to be a Spencer, and this room explains why.

The next room is perhaps the most startling, with its cine footage of Diana's childhood, shot lovingly by my father: her christening; her first winter; her first birthday; her first steps; her love of animals; her passion for swimming; her setting off for her first term at boarding school. When I first watched all the footage – and there was an enormous amount of it, from which four minutes were selected for the public – it was an incredibly harrowing experience. To watch these carefree times, with the willowy little girl delighting in life, and yet know what was to happen to her, thirty-odd years later, lent the screening all the elements of dramatic irony that I could live without.

At first I had hoped to edit it myself; but it was too personal, too draining. The job went to Tim Ashton, a London creative director, who has added a deeply moving music track to go with the film, down to the final flickering of the frame, as it freezes on Diana at her happiest and most humorous.

The third room deals with the glamour and excitement of the Royal Wedding, the dress taking centre stage, as well as many other mementoes of that portentous day in 1981.

From there, it is on to a space dedicated to Diana's charitable and humanitarian work, underlining why people appreciated her, and stressing the arduous nature of her working life. A film is shown on three screens, simultaneously; sometimes with the same images on all three and at other times with different ones appearing, to capture the volume and variety of work achieved by Diana in her public life. Testimonies from her charities to her extraordinary effect on their morale, bank balances, staff and recipients adorn the walls.

On into the Tribute Room, an evocation of those doom-laden days between Diana's death and burial, when the public were reduced to shocked silence in their attempt to digest the death of a much-loved icon. Here is another Tim Ashton-edited video, and other items, including the original text of my Tribute to Diana, written by me in the early hours of the Wednesday following her death. It probably sounds pompous, but it was a privilege to deliver it for her, in the way I know she would have wanted it.

We want to celebrate Diana's life, and not just mourn her death, so the final room – the main one in the Stables – is made over to her glamour, with huge glass cases displaying her finest clothes; again, in context and not simply as a fashion parade. As the visitors pass these, their eyes will be drawn to the huge glass case at the end: the resting place of just a few hundred of the many thousands of condolence books from around the world, banked one on top of the other, giving a final sense of scale to the impact of Diana's life and of her death.

Outside, the Park and gardens have been adapted by Dan Pearson, one of Britain's foremost garden designers, and another youthful member of the team. First, he crafted a walk from the car park through the

The final room in the Exhibition, a celebration of Diana's life.

West Lodge to the Stables, that could inspire, as well as give a sense of arrival. Thirty-six oaks were planted in an avenue, to signify the years Diana lived, with limes being added to beautify the area further. Ten thousand plants were used around the areas that will be seen by visitors, including 100 white rambling roses on the island where she was buried, and 1,000 white water lilies, donated by Stowe School, in the water itself.

Around the edge of the Oval, large benches were placed for people to sit and contemplate, designed by Dan to look more like fallen logs than the sort of garden furniture that might be expected in such a setting. Between the path and the water, fresh turf was laid, to replace the unkempt grass that had previously been there, giving Dan the chance to soften the gradient, so enabling the public to sit there on dry days. In all, around the lake and its approaches, enough turf to lay six football pitches has been used.

Next to the lake stands a small temple. In 1901 the Red Earl was at the end of a period as First Lord of the Admiralty during one of Gladstone's premierships. It was a position that he enjoyed far more than any of the others he had received during his years as a politician, and he was keen to have a memento of this period of his life.

When he learned that the two summer houses of the Admiralty Garden were to be disposed of, he bought the larger one – the Temple – for £3, and had it transported to the side of the Round Oval. It has family significance beyond this, having been a favourite retreat of George John, the Second Earl, when he in turn became First Lord of the Admiralty.

Now I had Edward Bulmer design something fitting for Diana, using the Temple as a focal point. This would be where the public could lay

their floral tributes. There was also to be a bench inside, thoughtfully donated by the Estate, for use by the family in private, during the ten months per year when the Park would be closed.

In the centre, at the front of the Temple, is a silhouette of Diana, in black marble on a white marble background. Henry Holland would have approved of the material used, marble being a favourite of his. Either side are tablets, one with a quote from Diana about her readiness to do charitable work, the other the conclusion of my Tribute at Westminster Abbey.

At the opposite end of the island from this is an urn, continuing the tradition of my family for erecting such structures in the Park to mark truly significant events. Before the island was a simple place of beauty, with its trees and rich undergrowth; now the urn, on its plinth, stands proud and noble, establishing this as the final resting place of a national heroine.

The memorial urn and plinth which mark Diana's burial place.

The Temple dedicated to Diana, where the public gather to pay their respects.

When I enter the gates of Althorp today, I feel an enormous sense of warmth, the classic Englishness of the Park enveloping me in its natural beauty, looking close to perfection at all times of year. I cannot decide whether it looks better in February, the trees' branches standing stark and frosted; in May, when the greens of the different leaves still have their contrasting hues; or in September, the thick sunlight in the heavy autumnal air.

One thing I am sure about: this is a special place. It has been home to such a diversity of interesting characters, each of whom has risen to the challenge of imparting some of their tastes to succeeding generations, making their mark, as I always feared I would never be able to make mine.

They were not necessarily 'great' people, these five centuries of Spencers; I would not pretend that they were. But they strike me, on balance, as having been good, and conscientious, and decent, with the odd rogue livening up the pages of the family's history from time to time. Above all, they had one thing in common: a love and appreciation of Althorp, in the unfashionable county of Northamptonshire, where they knew they were able to be truly at home, away from the pressures of the wider world.

Althorp House stands low, modest from the outside in all but size, more homely than stately; the repository of 500 years of collecting, of styles, of developing practicalities. It now has a place in history far greater than it ever achieved from its fleeting royal visits of earlier times; but I reckon the old place can cope, just as it has with everything else that has come its way, ever since we first grazed our herds here in the time of Henry Tudor.